THE

QUARTERLY

EDITED BY

GORDON LISH

Coifed and powdered
by Mr. Phyllis of Winnipeg

Hey, bet you're one of the persons whose work this magazine, in due portion, is. Good. We're on the right track. So let's suppose you're such a person and, as would only be natural for you to do, you went poking in a bookstore and therein discovered the sumbitches did not have the fucking Q you're in. Well, fine. Here is your chance to get modishly confrontational so that you get a headstart fitting right in with the whole mad end-of-century irascible thing. Okay: 1) Demand to see the manager/the owner/creature-in-charge, 2) Express your melancholy and shock at noting absence where presence belongs, 3) Allow as how the Gods of the National Literature are going to wax muy wroth indeed if Inland, our distributor, is not telephoned posthaste (at 1-800-243-0138—please to ask for Mr. Jared McCarthy) and the matter swiftly amended, 4) Given that you will have with you the edition of the Q you're in, shift field, be nice, and hurry to offer your interlocutor the numerals giving ISSN number and the ISBN number of the object in your hand. Swell. Now say thank you and go get yourself a Royal Mandarin Orange Almond Flake Bran Muffin in honor of a job well done.

Yours in gratitude, the kids in Suite 2600

But whatever you do, take no shit from nobody. You're in the right. Zeus is on your side. So is history. If worse comes to worst, get whoever's hassling you to call Sam Hiyate at the Toronto telephone number printed on the copyright page, which is one of the pages up here in the front of the mag with all the teensy-tiny print on it. Sam's the man. He'll hassle the hell out of whoever it is right back.

THE
QUARTERLY

29 / SPRING 1995

GUTTER PRESS

THE ROSENKRANZ FOUNDATION

TORONTO • NEW YORK

THE QUARTERLY (ISSN: 0893-3103) IS EDITED BY GORDON LISH
AND IS BROUGHT OUT IN JANUARY, APRIL, JULY, AND OCTOBER
AT SUITE 100, 50 BALDWIN STREET, TORONTO, ONTARIO M5T 1L4
(TEL: 416-977-7187; FAX: 416-861-8804) AT $10 U.S. THE COPY
AND $12 CANADIAN. SUBSCRIPTION REQUESTS (FOUR ISSUES AT
$30 U.S., $36 CANADIAN, AND $40 U.S. OVERSEAS),
ORDERS OF BACK COPIES, AND ALL OTHER BUSINESS MATTERS PLEASE ADDRESS TO THE
ABOVE, WHEREAS EDITORIAL TRANSACTIONS SHOULD BE DIRECTED TO SUITE 2600,
650 MADISON AVENUE, NEW YORK, NY 10022 (TEL: 212-888-4769).

MANAGING EDITORS : JODI DAVIS, DANA SPIOTTA
DESIGN : ANDREW ROBERTS
TYPOGRAPHY : PETER ANDERSEN
COPY CHIEF : JEN FLEISSNER
COPY ASSISTANTS : CHRISTOPHER MCDERMOTT, BRENDAN KOERNER
PRODUCTION ASSISTANTS : RUSSELL BERLAND, M. KRISTIN BEARSE, JOY NEWTON
PUBLICISTS : V. G. DAWSON, SARAH THRING
CIRCULATION MANAGER : KATHLEEN HICKEY
PRINT PRODUCTION : JOHN DEGEN, PETER MCCALLUM
PRINTERS and BINDERS : STAN BEVINGTON, JOHN DEJESUS, COACH HOUSE PRINTING
PUBLISHER : SAM HIYATE   EMAIL : shiyate@alias.com

THE QUARTERLY WELCOMES THE OPPORTUNITY TO READ WORK OF EVERY
CHARACTER, AND IS ESPECIALLY CONCERNED TO KEEP ITSELF AN OPEN FORUM.
MANUSCRIPTS MUST BE ACCOMPANIED BY THE CUSTOMARY RETURN MATERIALS
OR NOTIFICATION DEVICE. THE MAGAZINE MAKES THE UTMOST EFFORT TO
OFFER ITS RESPONSE TO MANUSCRIPTS NO LATER THAN ONE WEEK SUBSEQUENT
TO RECEIPT. OPINIONS EXPRESSED HEREIN ARE NOT NECESSARILY THOSE
OF THE EDITOR OR OF THE PUBLISHER.

COVER AND COLOPHON BY CHIP KIDD

ISBN : 0-9696520-9-7

LOTS OF MAIL'S BEEN SHOWING UP IN EXPRESSION OF A STATE OF CONSTERNATION
(NEVER USE ONE LATINATE SUFFIX WHEN YOU CAN USE TWO!) CONCERNING
THE INTENTION (OR THREE!) OF THIS PUBLICATION (FOUR!—AND SURELY MORE
THAN ENOUGH TO HOLD YOU AND YOUR WHOLE FAMILY FOR THE DURATION—
WHOOPS, FIVE!—OF THE SENTENCES PLANNED FOR THIS SPACE). PEOPLE, SOME
OF THEM ACTUALLY CANADIANS NOT UNNATURALLY (HAH!), WONDER ALOUD
WHAT THE FUCK WE THINK WE'RE UP TO, WONDERMENT NOT WITHOUT
AN ORIGIN IN GOOD SENSE. THE INQUIRY CAN BE REPLIED TO IN A HOST
A MANNERS, CAN IT NOT? WE MIGHT SAY, FOR EXAMPLE, AND QUITE COMPLETELY
IN EARNEST, THAT OUR HOPE IS TO PRODUCE A MAGAZINE UNIQUE AMONG
MAGAZINES. OR, FOR FURTHER EXAMPLE, WE MIGHT TAKE THE LINE THAT
WE HAVE NO IDEA WHAT WE'RE DOING. BUT IT IS PROBABLY BEST TO MAKE
THE CLAIM THAT THE Q SEEKS FOR THOSE WHOSE EFFORTS CONTRIVE
IT A PLACE FOR SUCH EFFORTS TO BE FREE OF THE AUTHORITY
OF THE PRECEDENTED. SO OUR QUESTION TO THE CONSTERNATED IS THIS—
"WITH SO MUCH ROOM TO MAKE USE OF, HOW COME SO MANY FOLKS
ALL KEEP HUDDLING IN THE SAME CORNER?"

MANUFACTURED IN CANADA

THE QUARTERLY

29 / WINTER 1994

THE QUARTERLY

(Oh shit, l left out Rita Dove!)

As an interning production assistant here
at this here magazine, l Russell Berland,
in the great spirit of the great Harold
Bloom, respectfully wish to submit to
you, our friends, this here magazine's
readers', the Western Cannon as l,
Russell Berland, know it truly to be:
1) Barbara Bradford Taylor – Hold the
Dream and the Women In His Life
2) Danielle Steele – To Love Again and
Summer's End 3) Anything about
Vampires! 4) ~~Anything by E.L. Doctorow~~
4) Gore Vidal, Gore Vidal, Gore Vidal,
(Gosh, l feel smart just saying it)!!
("this word is reader's") ("this word is smart")

Fuck, another one, there's another one l
forgot, which is The Flight to Lucifer,
which is the novel penned by the
maestro himself, Prof. Bloom, Or it
could maybe be it's called The Flight
From Lucifer. Anyway, Whatever the
Prof. called it! It's the fucking tops,
You know?

Nötrë Pënsëës

You won't believe it! I, Patty [1980-] did not myself believe it! But it's true, it's true! You know about the famous French philosopher Julia Kristeva? Okay, she is probably not as totally famous as the American philosopher Camille Paglia is —but, come on, let's face it, who is? Anyway, this is what Julia said to me, Patty [1980-]. She said, "Look, Patty [1980-], gal to gal, how come you call your column "Our Thoughts" when it's just you who write down the thoughts?" In other words, as I, Patty [1980-] interpret Julia's question, if it is just me who writes down the thoughts, then how come I say "our" instead of saying "my"? Because like to say "our" instead of saying "my" is like saying these thoughts are the thoughts not just of just me personally but also of other people besides me. Anyway, this is my personal interpretation of what Julia's question

*is trying to say, and I, Patty [1980-], happen to think my
interpretation of it is a very good interpretation even if people could say I myself, Patty [1980-] am not a philosopher personally. So, listen, if you have a good tough one like
that one was which you would like to ask me, then go ahead
and do it. Just send your question along to me and I will
answer it once I have taken a good look at it and got it in-
terpreted correctly. But don't ask me the same question Julia
just did because I already have been asked it. Ask me a new
one so I can really go to town on it. Like you could ask me
what kind of a human being I think Doug is for his yank-
ing his fucking money out from under me and trying to cut
the heart out of this operation, which is probably the only
deal in this whole stinking fucking stupid magazine which
makes the least little bit of sense. Love and kisses, and that
goes double from me to you, Camille! You're so snazzy and
savvy and sassy! You're all spunk—and I, Patty [1980-]
sure am nutsy-crazy about you. Hey, I bet you could duke it out
with old Julia any old day there ever was!* PATTY [1980-].

HANG ON! HOLD IT! JESUS GODDAMN CHRIST, YOU WON'T BELIEVE IT! BUT SOMEBODY FOUR
THOUSAND YEARS YOUNGER THAN ANYBODY'S OLD AUNT ALLIE JUST CAME IN THE DOOR
HERE WITH A CHECK THAT IT WOULD KILL YOU IF YOU COULD SEE THE SIZE OF IT. BEST OF ALL,
SHE DEMANDS ANOMIMI . . . NO, AMONYME . . . SHE SAYS (TINY ALICIA SAYS) WOE BETIDE THE
LITMAG BASTARDO WHO SPILLS THE BEANS ABOUT WHAT MY NAME IS.

Another Litmag the Q
Is Better Than
and Why

Okay, we give up.
It's true, *Harper's* is a better litmag.
It's got more lit.
It's got more mag.
It doesn't even have perfume in it,
which is something to really stand up and shout about.
Well, okay, you never know,
it could be like it's got some kind of
very light toilette water in it maybe.
It could be like it's this really subtle stuff
which you can't really smell or anything
unless your nose is in just the right position
for it, but then this probably gets your eyes
out of position so you can't like be reading probably,
which, granted, is a terrific problem,
but, hey, isn't *Harper's*
worth it?

THE

QUARTERLY

I had expected
more dramatic results

Correspondence

Dear K,

I told her once, "You are so entirely without surprises." How surprised she would be by my writing to ask this of you. What I am asking of you will not be difficult for you to do. Is it not something you have already done? But I am not asking you to do exactly what you did to her. That was only a rehearsal, as it were, and she the understudy. Besides, I do not know exactly what you did do, although I know, perhaps, more than you think. You and she and God are the only ones who know what happened all those years ago. At all events, she was not the one worthy of such a death.

I presume it was not difficult for you. It probably came upon you of a sudden, as they say. Perhaps there was a moment of exhilaration, something approaching ecstacy, a moment when you felt more alive than you had ever done before. Probably you thought of it as the supreme embrace. You, certainly, were very thorough. Certain scenes from literature come to mind. But you would not know anything about those, would you?

You must have guessed that this would be something I would have wanted. It must be something you, for as long a time, have wanted to do. I have always felt you understood my actual desires. Did you not once say how alike we are? We even look alike. Like brother and sister, in fact, whereas she and I looked like strangers, I expect. At best she looked like a pale copy of the original; the negative. I have a portrait of us as little girls—one of those sentimental renderings, made of children of that class in those days. It hangs above my desk in a heart-shaped beaten silver frame. She has her arm about my waist, I, mine about her neck. She smiles up at me with her forget-me-not eyes. Her pallid complexion. Her white-tipped eyelashes. The child-white hair.

I woke last night in this large half-empty room. Yes, yes, it occurred to me you must have taken her by surprise. Did she have a chance to cry out? What did she say? Was it in the light or in   shadow? Did you know these are the questions she used to ask me about the act of making love? She was always asking me about the act of making love. I knew more than she did about that, naturally. She wanted to know how long it took, if one suffered, if one talked; and if so, what one said. If I, for example, left a light burning.

You must realize she talked to me. Sometimes we sat up huddled together in that hot room under the eaves. She would talk to me all through the night. Of course she did not talk directly. But I could read between the lines. Inevitably, she would speak of you. Later, she wrote me letters. Occasionally, we spoke on the telephone. Some of what she told me amazed me. Some of it I would rather not have known. But I asked questions. I even gave her advice. But she, I gather, took half-measures. You do not take half-measures. You have taken all. You like surprises, don't you? Yes—you like surprises.

When Mother called me with the news, I was not surprised. Mother sounded angry. I said something about the endless voyage out. Spoke of the plane ride, of the dreadful ferry crossing from the mainland to the island, the boat black with soot, the seas rough at that time of year. "Don't come then," she said.

I said, "I must, of course, come."

When I told my husband, he turned to me with his habitual courtesy of attitude and said in his sweet voice, "How did he manage it?"

You will understand how easily I could manage this.

I have planned the thing in detail.

Unlike her, I like to plan.

Let me tell you what you need to know. A person can come and go like a ghost here. The house, one of a row of identical townhouses, is situated on a dead-end street. It is very quiet except for the hour when the children escape from school. These flat, ashen townhouses face the public gardens imperturbably in this most provincial of French settings. The window panes are small. They look east and west. But there are none on the sides of the house. The dwelling itself is divided in half, with separate entrances, front and back, linked by a long dark corridor. Once it was two separate houses, so that the floor slopes a little as you go along it. All of this dates from the last century. The big rooms have high ceilings, thick walls with heavy moldings—patisseries, my husband calls them. My rooms are at the back; this is where I work, and where I lie down at night. I do not sleep much, of course, unlike her, who was always sleeping. I leave the lamp lit and read, or just lie here thinking about my work for the next day, or I stare at the ceiling, watch a shadow shift. These rooms are quite satisfactory, very different from those brilliantly lit rooms with their open windows and open doors and thin walls where we grew up. Here it is very different—very, shall I say, discreet?

The back entrance is the way to my rooms. It is through a small iron gate with a secret fastening. The trick is simple. All you have to do is to slip your hand through the bars and under the creeper and lift the lever gently from the inside. This will take you into the back-garden. My rooms look over the damp silent back-garden, lit at best with wan sunlight or by the ghostly light of the moon. Today there is no sunlight at all but snow, the first snowfall of the season. Light flakes fall straight from a white sky. Smoke billows upward from the gray chimneys like a field of white blooms. The garden is swallowed up by snow. A lip of snow lies on the window sill.

My husband inherited all this from his ancestors, who were Bretons from the *petite noblesse*. His ancestors are buried with the kings of France, you know; *chiens couchants* at their feet. My husband has, for my edification, explained many times and at length the differences among the nobilities.

Perhaps you are worrying about my husband?

What if he should be in the vicinity?

You will understand that he is not often in the vicinity. He receives his patients in the front rooms of the house; I work in the back. We each spend our days listening. He listens to the murmur of hearts, lungs, joints. I harken to morphemes and the like. What I spend most of my days doing is translating. I do French, Italian, Spanish. Lately I have taken up Hungarian. I have always thought Baudelaire's version of Poe far superior to the original. I do not feel obliged to keep strictly to the words before me, just as when you come to me to do what you must realize I am asking, I, her sister, will allow you certain imaginative departures from the procedure you employed the last time.

According to Mother, they found her unclothed body in the shade of the tamarind trees. Mother said it was pleasantly cool under the trees at dusk. She said a slight breeze was blowing in the long grass. It was the buzzing of the flies, she said, that alerted her to the presence of the body. A swarm of flies had already settled on the reeking wounds. How expectable; the kind of pale soft skin that attracts mosquitoes and flies. How fitting that she should have found it, do you not think?

Here we will not have to bother with flies or insects of any kind. It is too cold for mosquitoes. Besides, such vermin have always kept their distance from me.

Hah, but not to take me for some silkworm spinning a cocoon of silken lies to envelope you and bring about your metamorphosis. You are not the sort of person one lies to, are you? You are far too clever. I do not need to dispossess you to entice you into my territory. I need you just as you are, as the song goes. Just as you need me.

Oh, do not construe this correspondence as the musings of an overheated imagination. Count on my good sense. Unlike her, my motto is *festina lente*. I like to run behind a faster runner, shelter in her shadow until the end is in sight. Then I pass my quarry by. I like sunlight filtered through shutters, dappled light through leaves; I like concealment.

I accuse no one of anything, you realize. I judge no one.

The time to come to me would be night. I retire to my rooms early. We never eat lunch but work until late afternoon, when we trot a bit around the public gardens. We circle them, our greyhound loping at our heels. Can you see the chestnut trees spreading thin branches against the white sky? In the distance the children sail toy boats. The band plays a waltz. We proceed one behind the other in our identical white hats, our gaze lowered to the stones at our feet. My husband prefers the landscape produced in Art. He never looks at things and, particularly, does not admire flowers. Even my photo, which he keeps on his desk in his consulting rooms, is one in which I am seen from behind.

We prepare a light supper, usually spaghetti in *bianco* or a grilled fish fillet followed by poached fruit, in silence. The fellow is usually silent except with the dog. We never quarrel; we are always extremely polite. In the evenings in the kitchen—a narrow shadowy room with a stone floor and stone countertops scrubbed with *savon de Marseilles*, and rudimentary plumbing—we vie with one another to cook the evening meal, moving around the narrow room like twin ghosts, skirting one another, mumbling to ourselves; he mumbles in French, I in English. Occasionally, I let things slip through my fingers. Once, I let slip a good china pitcher that had belonged to his mother. He uttered not a word. This morning, too, as I heard him gashing with a knife to retrieve the last drop of jam from the jar, I put out my hand to take the knife from him. There was never a sign of rebuke, reproach, or the slightest displeasure.

We eat our supper on trays before the television while we watch the evening news. Sometimes he touches my hand, and he will sigh, a glimmer, I think, of hope in his pale blue eyes. But each night I take the plunge alone, unarmed, naked, into that ocean where we meet the dead. It is not necessary to lock my door. Do you see how easily you could come to me?

You came that very first time at dusk, the sun at your back. By chance I was watching from the window on the staircase. You walked up the driveway as though you were a tall man. Your clothes seemed strange: too tight in places, too loose in others. You gave me the impression of coming from some other land, an alien. You had the arrogance she so admired, though I am not sure what it is that seems to give you this quality. I watched you emerging from the sunset wood, standing under the double row of tamarinds, where, of course, she was to die. I saw you gazing across the hills recumbent in the last of the light. The air was still. There was no wind. I watched you as you studied the house. There was a peculiar smile, I thought. The moths followed you into the hall. I could hardly see your face in the shadows. Perhaps you were looking at the disarray of flowers and baskets and vases on the table there, Mother's half-finished pyramid of peonies and pinks in the soup tureen, or perhaps at the floor that was red and shiny from the wax they rubbed into the ochre. I heard you tell the servant that you had come about the advertisement. I stood at the door at the top of the steps to the lounge and listened to your conversation with Mother and Aunt Maude. I remember Mother putting down her porcelain cup and leaning toward you, an elbow on her knee, saying something about wanting her daughters to have the advantages she had never had. You said, "Daughters?" did you not? and Mother replied, "Two daughters," and sighed and said what she always did about the difficulty of bringing up two little girls on her own.

I remember your saying thoughtfully, "Ah, two," and adding that you could supply several languages, much in the way of mathematics, and a certain intimacy with music.

Mother went on as she always did about her never having had the opportunities, about her various deprivations, her disappointments, whereas it was Aunt Maude who interrupted to inquire as to your references.

I waited for you to respond.

I recall how you lifted your head and sniffed slightly and remarked on the luxurious presence in the house.

Mother nattered on about the abundance of honeysuckle and jasmine that cover the glassed-in sun porch.

That was when you walked indolently across the soft carpet to the Steinway by the French doors and opened the curtains a little. Your timing was *parfait*, I thought.

You always wore black, did you not?

Do you still wear black?

Surely black is rather hot for the tropics?

I watched as you opened the curtains a little to let in the light on the keys, adjusted the tapestried bench slightly, leaned back your head as though listening.

I was struck by the fact that your hair seemed almost too black, your complexion too smooth, your teeth too white.

What the regularity of your face made me think of was a mask. We all waited while the moment gathered.

Was it Rachmaninov you played? How old were you then? How many years later did you do it to her?

My husband's ancestors died for the French kings, you know, fighting against the English for a hundred years; they died in their heavy armor, sunk in the mud at Agincourt, and then they went on dying for the crown in the revolutionary wars. They were captured and drowned in pairs, tied back to back or face to face, the bottom of the boat opening up beneath their feet.

Sometimes, when we were younger, she would try to imitate my walk, holding herself erect, lifting her soft chin.

But only our voices could be confused, nothing else.

I see her face.

I see the ankles and wrists broken, the hands fingerless.

I see you coming toward me.

Listen to me—I shall have what I shall have. **Q**

GARY LUTZ

The Boy

The boy was raised in a city that had the look and feel of a state capital but in fact was not even a county seat. The buildings, big brutish granite piles, gave everybody the wrong idea. Travelers would see the castellated skyline from the highway, sheer off at the exit, park their cars, and climb steep steps to what they hoped, despite the absence of signs and plaques, would prove to be a mint or a museum. Once inside, they would find themselves in a cramped, fusty living room. Somebody—an old woman in a housecoat—would look up from a sofa and say, "Let a person sleep." The boy himself, on the other hand, did not have the look and feel of anything big or promising. You couldn't look up his name in books. Even as a child, he was always several removes from himself. Wherever he stood—near the swing set on a playground, for instance—he was never inarguably there, but his absence was always first-hand. His absence was, in fact, so commanding, so convincing, that the people around him were often confused about just exactly where they, too, stood. Obviously, his parents must have caught on very early to the un-exampled form of ventriloquism the boy had evolved, a ventriloquism that entailed displacing his entire flute-thin body, and they made the necessary adjustments—sudden half-steps or about-faces—in their own strides. That's why people thought they walked funny, that's why people thought they looked funny together as a family.

One day when the boy was ten years old, his father sat at the kitchen table soldering together two wires on the boy's tape recorder. The boy was sitting at the table, too, positioning and repositioning the saliva in his mouth, first behind one cheek and then behind the other, before swallowing.

The father could hear the sloshing sounds.

The tape recorder was the old reel-to-reel type.

The father was not especially good with his hands. In fact, the soldering iron—the risks that its use introduced into his life—terrified him. More important, the father was unforgiving. He was so unforgiving that he gave in time after time, doing everything for the boy out of a big, banging spite. With every splenetic dab of the soldering iron, the father thought he was disallowing the syllogism that runs: father, mother, son.

The boy was convinced that with his saliva he was accomplishing something very similar.

Walking home from the high school he attended at the other end of the city, the boy would often linger in a park near the tallest buildings. Crestfallen tourists would occasionally approach him. Once, a long-throated, heavily talcumed woman asked, "Have you a pen on your person?" The boy slued around slowly and exaggeratedly, as if to see whether there was a third party involved, an attendant bearing supplies. There was only his own angled, outbound body and, at a respectable distance, her own, a globulet of a tear glissading down her cheek. The woman moved on. There were plenty of men in the park whose pockets were full of pens and whatever else might be asked for.

One day during his eleventh-grade history class, the boy was summoned to the guidance counselor's office. The guidance counselor was a blocky, short-winded man with corned teeth and an overexerted vocabulary. He explained that to the best of his knowledge it would be in the best interest of both the boy and the school if, for the remainder of his tuition, he were enrolled as a girl. He explained that the boy's parents had already been informed and that papers had already been drawn up and dispatched for them to sign. That night, the mother took the boy shopping for a jumper, a white blouse, and pumps. The boy became very popular at school, excelled at all his subjects to the extent that was then expected of girls, and had many boyfriends, all of whom he did his best to please. At the commencement ceremony, the guidance counselor delivered a long speech about the boy and his progress. The speech was full of words like "miracle" and "rapture" and "angels." During the peroration, the guidance counselor publicly proposed to the boy. They were married a week later in an elaborate but rushed ceremony, during which the minister looked content in the knowledge that this smell would cover up that smell and so forth down the line, dominowise. Two weeks later, the guidance counselor died loudly and tumultuously in his sleep. The boy slipped out of the nightgown he was wearing and threw on an old robe and slumped across the dark city to his parents' house.

With his diploma and a cajoling, loopily handwritten application letter, the boy was offered a job 342 miles to the right of his bed if he was facing the wall that had the window, his favorite position. He rented a room, sight unseen, over the phone.

A week before the boy had to leave, his mother decided he needed a rug. She drove him to a carpet store to look at remnants.

The boy saw the salesman slide a cherry cough drop into his mouth from the box in his shirt pocket.

"You certainly know your way around in here," the salesman eventually said to the boy.

The boy turned away and paged through some carpet samples bound together in a book.

"I was saying, ma'am, that your son here has spent a lot of time in this store," the salesman said.

"We need something for the floor," the mother said.

"Okay," the salesman said. "What are we talking about?"

"It's just one big room," the mother said.

"How big of a room?" the salesman said.

The mother looked at her son. "How big a room?"

The boy did not answer.

"It's in Pennsylvania," the mother said.

There is an explanation for patricide that works in every case. In every case, there is a Coke machine close at hand.

The boy was always thirsty. The boy was always walking across the street to the machine, buying one can at a time, carrying it back to his room to drink at the table. The father was in town only for a visit. The greasy whorls of the father's thumbprints had already blurred the cover of the hobby magazine the boy had bought for the father to leaf through. Also on the table was an iron that the boy was convinced was prowling in a different direction each time he returned from the machine.

"You drink way too much Coke," the father said, finally.

"I'm thirsty," the boy said.

"Then drink water."

"I hate water."

"Coke don't even quench your thirst. Look at all the money you're wasting."

"If it doesn't quench my thirst, then tell me what it does do."

"It makes the inside of your mouth and throat nice and cold for a couple seconds. That's it. Water could do just as good."

The boy and his father sat and wordlessly pushed their points.

The knife presented itself to the boy as if in shimmery italics. The boy could not remember ever having bought it. It was a heftless, nervous-atomed, self-disowning simulacrum of what a knife was supposed to look like in a low-slung town.

As on so many occasions, this was the boy's first time, but everything rang a bell—a cracked, mootish, spanging bell. Each chink of it, each clank of it brought him a clangorous bit closer to the understood "you." **Q**

The Smell of How the World Had Ground Itself onto Somebody Else

From what I gather, I had to have had the sense, sooner or later, to get up and have a look at the outline my body had pressed into the carpet during sleep—the clearing I had made by pushing aside clothes and food wrappers and newspapers and such—and it could not have resembled the shape of any of the familiar postures of convalescence, because I remember thinking there were still some people, two or three people —I kept adding them together differently—who could be counted on, if reached at the right time of the month, to say, "I was just thinking about you," and these were not the people I thought to call.

The phone was one more constant thing on the floor—an old rotary-dial model with a dumbbell handset. I must have called the woman and hung on every word of mine, taken in everything I was saying, because I put clothes on and drove to the address I had repeated aloud when it was the first thing spelled out for me to write down.

She was living with her oldest brother and his blind cats and porcelain dolls in a rented rowhouse. The brother could have been out—either at the resort where he worked or at the school he had to go to. I probably asked about everybody else, just to make sure there was conversation, or just to be rooting for somebody, or why would I now swear that her two youngest (girl, girl) were with an aunt and her two oldest (boy, girl) were renting places of their own? What other reason would I have to bring any of them up? Wasn't I the one they claimed had told them things about the human body that could not possibly be true—that it was the grave the heart was buried in, and other misrepresentations of far worse ilk?

A doctor who liked the woman had written out a whole pad's worth of prescriptions, dated at two-month intervals, for a cone-

shaped junior tranquilizer, and as a believer in keeping something on my stomach, I am certain I must have taken what was
offered and chewed it. And then the woman had to have said,
"Come under the cuzzers," because I had only ever gone by
what was visible, the parts of things that stuck right out, and what
I was seeing was familiar—everything on her that gaped.

Her family, her children, knew where to find her when it
seemed reasonable to move back in. It took a couple of days. The
house—this was a differently addressed one, with shutters—had
three floors. Every room was going to have the same kind of
blinds. Everybody who was old enough to work was going to be
told how long, in weeks, they had in order to find a job. Names
and deadlines were going to get written on a kitchen wall that
was going to get painted harvest gold. The woman was making
good money and did not have to report to anybody except her
boss, who liked her and said, "No need to come in today—just
stay by that bonny phone of yours just in case."

At the time of which I write, my early forties, people were expected to provide their own transportation. The car I owned was
not presentable. It did not make an impression. One morning I
drove to a used-car dealership and stood at the edge of the lot.
Within an hour the salesman had me cleaning out my trunk and
my back seat. It had to be done with great haste, he said. A
woman was already interested in the car, he said. He wheeled
over two large garbage barrels, then dragged out some cardboard boxes to hold whatever I was going to keep. He said he
understood what it must be like to live in a small place and have
nowhere to go with your things.

It was the woman and the oldest daughter who afterward
pretended to be attorneys and made the lawyerly threats over
the phone to the salesman, the sales manager, the president of
the lot. None of it did any good—once you sign a contract, etc.
The new car was a galling brick-red littleness in the woman's
gravelled driveway. I could look out the window and see her
youngest two peering into the windows of it, pointing at the

boxes that were too big for the trunk. The boxes did not yet belong in the house.

The oldest daughter kept saying, "I won't bite you." I listened from the other end of the living room when it was her turn to talk legal into the phone. To prolong her threats, she kept up a kind of vowelly crooning between words. It was the first I had ever taken much notice of her. She was in her twenties and had arranged the freckly lengthiness of her body into a slouch that made her elbows and legs seem pointed privately, inquiringly, toward me. I started siding with her, beholding whatever she beheld—the fishbowl ashtray, the dishful of pastilles and drops, the plum-colored splotch she kept rubbing on her shin.

As thanks, I said I would take the two of them, mother and oldest daughter, out to dinner, someplace decent and scarcely lit. The daughter went upstairs and took a long, decisive shower—I could hear all the water it was taking—and then came down in a slip and kneeled in front of the coffee table and looked up into my face as she applied the determining makeup.

At the restaurant she asked me questions about herself—what I thought she thought, which violences I considered her capable of—and no matter what I said, she would say, "That's a good answer," or "How right you always are."

"But you're so far away," she said, finally.

We were seated at a banquette, the daughter in the middle. The woman kept getting up to call her boss.

For maybe two or three nights after that, I fell asleep on my floor starting with the woman under my eyes, then adding on the two-inch advantage every generation supposedly gained over their parents, lightening and lengthening the hair, overpowdering the face, inflating the biceps, spattering freckles onto the arms and chest, until I had brought the daughter on top of me in her avid, breastless entirety.

As always, I was slow to let on I knew how far I was being taken advantage of. The daughter fell in with some friends of her brother's, tight-lipped teenagers in floppy shorts that came down to their shins. That was the last I saw of her for years.

One night I stupidly told the woman how I felt.

"That's all going to change," she said.

Instead, the woman opted for misery and hardship and unemployment of a high order. These were the years of learning disabilities, loosenesses of mind, downheavals all over. I went through her thick mail. I remember disconnection notices, policy cancellations, bounced-check statements, form letters declaring which child was suspended from school and for how long, collection-letter sequences whose initial entry always started with the question "Have You Forgotten Something?"

What I kept forgetting was that I was nothing to anybody under that roof other than the one who stuck around for it to repeatedly dawn on everybody else—her relations, mostly; the brother above all—that it takes all kinds.

In time, the oldest daughter came back. She arrived in a car of her own. Most of her hair was gone. This was the smallest house yet, a cottage. It was still daylight out on the porch. I could see that from the car the girl was looking into the uncurtained window, already figuring herself back onto the furniture.

"You were going to say something," she said in my direction. "You were going to put something to me," she said.

"A proposition," she said.

The woman had to step outside in her graphic housecoat and explain to the daughter that there was nowhere for the daughter to sleep.

I could describe the circles the other children left the house to move around within. I could describe the walks of life they applied themselves to lavishly. I could describe the beds they slept athwart. I would not be the first. There is already a beaten path.

The least I can say is that once in who knows how long you actually get to see where you are living. I can attest to this plentifully. I can speak from experience something awful. Just this once, you have the chance: all the right lights are finally on.

Your first thought is to let somebody else take over the talking. That summer the two of us rolled what was left of my pennies—there were still basinsful of them, drawersful that went all the way back to my youth—and I drove the woman to where there was one large body of water, and then on to where there was another, and then on yet again. There were always seagulls, a span of boardwalk, waves, shells to accumulate in our drinking cups. But it was never the sea, she claimed. Show me a sea, she said.

I was a thoroughgoer. There was so much to go back on.

Years must have gone by without my fingering getting any better. The woman kept saying: "A little lower."

Or: "Not even close."

Or: "Do you even know where you are?"

It says something about my wife, which is what the woman had become, that I am saying any of this so voluminously. Because if you are anything like me—*please be*—you have had the sense to keep yourself under investigation long enough to already know what is in store.

For instance, walking in on her when she is transferring everything from one handbag to the other.

Does she say: "Finish your meal"?

Or: "All you do is make work"?

Or: "Occupy yourself"?

In my case, there were only a couple of spots left for me to still fill. One was at work. This was the spot in which I had found out I was not being paid the same as everybody else. I was in the washroom, soaping my hands at the sink, when I heard my name come up in conversation in the stalls behind me. Whoever the voices belonged to had got hold of a printout of how much everybody was making. A distribution. I rinsed my hands and dried them on a paper towel and got out of there in one two three.

Later in life, I brought the matter up with a supervisor. I got called a malcontent, a troublemaker, more hindrance than help. What could she do but put me behind a desk even farther from the public? She took me off light-administrative and put me on time sheets. Work was brought to me in carts.

"Do your dirt on numbers for a change" is all the other one—the one who always gave straight answers—told me to my face.

One other spot I was in—the last of them—was the one at whose center I kept getting even worse at judging the distances between people. I fouled up every time. If I saw somebody declaring herself with a gesture, I intercepted as much as I could of whatever was on its way to whom it may have actually concerned. I helped myself to anything headed elsewhere. I carried on as if it were mine.

Do I have to draw a picture? The one I keep drawing and shoving in her face is the one of me walking home from work one day when she had the car. I passed a store where a kid was sitting along a landscaped strip that bordered the parking lot. The kid had its arms wrapped around its shins, knees pointing up.

"I cut myself," the kid said to me alone.

I stopped for a look. I saw a knee with a scab that looked picked-at. A few platelets of scab were loose and afloat in what little blood there was.

The scab was the color of ham. Burnt ham.

I took the clean handkerchief out of my back pocket, squatted next to the kid, patted the handkerchief against the knee. A few circlets of blood appeared on the face of the cloth.

I said something like: "Just keep that on there for a while."

And here comes what your life will never be the same after which, the same way mine had already never been: my face was bent right over the kid's other knee. The knee was aimed right at me.

I got a whiff of it, all right. I got the hell out of there.

Who hasn't lived his life expressly to avoid having to one day inhale something that entire? It was the complete, usurping smell of how the world had ground itself onto somebody else.

Did I hasten home and shut myself in the bathroom and try to bring forth a similar smell—something equally total—from my own knees? Did I wait until my wife had fallen asleep and then expect to drag its like out of hers? Did I slip out of bed and put my clothes back on, let myself out of the house, steer a straight course toward the parking lot at the store, roll up the legs of my pants, grind my kneecaps into the damp earth until the dirt was caked onto the flesh, then roll the pants down again, plunge home, sneak into the bathroom, disrobe, remount the toilet, bury my nose in my knee, and draw in big hopeful breath-gulps to satisfy myself that the disrupting magnificence on the kid's knee—the alarm—had been nothing more than the neglected pressing smellsomeness of dirt alone; and having discovered, instanter, that it was not a matter of dirt, that the point of origin—of contact—lay elsewhere, did I spend the next couple of weeks before and after supper wending my way around the purlieus of the store, the alleys and backyards and traffic islands, keeping my gait brisk and neighborish, doing my best to preserve the appearance of an unprovoked, unprowling fellow in walking shorts first working up an appetite, then strolling off his meal, but always, ultimately, futilely, rubbing the knees against something differently frictional—tree bark or smoothed rock, the blacktop of a driveway or nettles in a vacant lot?

Did I ever once in all of this time bring off anything remotely approximating a get-together with my wife? Did it eventually occur to me to seek out the kid itself? Did I have any luck? Did I have enough sense to burst into my supervisor's office and make a clean breast of it? Did I say: "This is what I've done. This is what I'm doing. This is what I will have done by the time I am finished"? Because if people should happen to ask, it will be only because they are sick of being pestered for the answer. The identical let-down looks on their faces are the only way the hostess can tell for sure the people are all in the same party the one time it occurs to them to venture out to eat as a community.

So go ahead.

Make anything up.

Tell them whatever their little hearts desire.

Tell them I was an only son at the time the world was filling up with women, making everything harder for me to see. **Q**

Street Map of the Continent

Some days his work took him into people's houses. He would enter a room, part the air, odor things differently, then come out with whatever it was. Never a word of thanks from anybody, but they would usually ask if he needed to use the bathroom—a powder room, more often than not. He would picture them listening to the flushes, counting.

He lived with a woman who volunteered at the library and brought a different book home every night. She would sit with it open on her lap and work the tip of an uncrooked paper clip into the gutter where the facing pages met, prying things loose: fingernail peelings, eyebrow hairs, pickings and outbursts and face- scrapings. Anything on the plane of the page itself—the immediate heedless presence of the previous reader in the form of abundances of shed hair, say, or gray powderings of scalp—she swept onto the floor. She evacuated the books, then ran the vacuum cleaner. In the morning, the book went back to the library.

The man had his own chair and watched her like a hawk.

There were a few years of cordial intimacy with the woman, and then her teeth began to lose their way in her gums. They listed and slid. The sticky hair she always combed into a canopy over her forehead started to droop, and the color went dim. Her eyes seemed to take him in less and less.

One morning she was nowhere the man could see. Most of the clothes she had liked were gone, too.

He called in sick.

He sat in his chair watching the kitchen from the hour when the table was a breakfast table to the hour when it was a supper table.

He started buying newspapers—anything he could get his hands on, one of each. There were some that came out only once a week and printed the menus of the senior-citizen high-rises in town. These the man tore out and taped to the refrigerator door.

The grocery store where he bought the papers was not part of a chain. The floor dipped and sloped. The aisles started out as ample causeways, veered off, then narrowed down to practically nothing. There were vitrines back there. Display cases. Nobody seemed particular about what went into them. The man started bringing things to add.

Her shoes, with the gloating, mouthy look that shoes acquire when no longer occupied.

Her stockings, riveled and unpleasant to touch.

Sheet after sheet of her swaying penmanship.

Numbers she had piled high onto graph paper.

One night he called the home number of the man who lined up the jobs for him.

"Yes," the voice said, over TV noise.

He put the phone down. Her smoking and sewing tackle were on the telephone stand. He put them in a bag to take to the store.

The sleeplessness spread to his arms and his legs. He practiced removing her absence from one place and parking it somewhere else. There was too much furniture in the house, he decided.

The town was one whose name the citizens had never had to spell out on the envelope when paying a bill or sending a card locally. Instead, they could just write *City*. Then came a generation who grew up suspecting there were two different places—one a town, the other a city—with the same set of streets and addresses. These people were less sure of where they lived and spent too much time deciding whether the shadows that fell across sidewalks and playgrounds were too big or too little for whatever the shadows were supposed to be shadows of. These were people who dreamed of towers that would never quite stay built even in dreams.

Depending on which sources the man read, he could be counted as part of either generation.

The only other thing ever known about him was that when it came time to take his car in for the annual inspection, he sat in a little waiting area off to the side of the garage. A mechanic came in and told him that they had gone ahead and put a sticker on the car, but there were oral disclaimers about the brakes, the tires. "I don't know what kind of driving you do," the mechanic said. "Is it mostly around here, or highway?"

"Highway," the man said.

Weeks went by before he thought to stop. **Q**

Onesome

To get even with myself on behalf of my wife, to see how far I had been putting her out, I began to ingurgitate my own seed. I had to go through with everything twice the first night because it came out initially as thin as drool and could not have possibly counted as punishment. The next time—I had let an hour or so elapse—some beads of it clung to a finger, and a big mucousy nebula spread itself into the bowl of my palm. By the time I got everything past my lips, much of it had already cooled, but I revolved the globules around in my mouth slowly, deservedly, several times before allowing myself a swallow. There turned out to be nothing clotty or gagging about it—why, then, her gripes, her grudges?—just a bitter stickiness that stayed put.

I repeated everything in the morning and again before bed. I began to hear—or imagine—a glueyness, a tightness, in things I now said. It made me think twice about opening my mouth.

Is it news to anybody that my wife had already given up on me hand and foot? She wanted her own room, and she got it, the small one downstairs we had never settled on any lasting purpose for. I went along, knowing how little it takes for a room to become the opposite of room.

Let me ask myself something else: should a father and his daughter have to fear each other tit for tat? Did I not make sure the door to her room was open when I made polite bedtime conversation with her? There was a prolixity of purple-blue veins legible beneath her skin, and on her face I could see my own features garbled, corrected, redressed. Childhood had accumulated in her and was getting ready to sour into something far worse. She had her own secret life and a circlet of friends who all had nearly the same name—Loren, Lorene, Lorena, I could never get them all straight. She was a decent kid—picked up after herself, got high marks in the hardest subjects. I had no bone to pick with her except she kept breathing down my crotch and then expected me to provide the food, the clothing, the shelter she needed to rule me out for good.

Marriage is what—the most pointless distance between two points? Or the foulest? Which?

My earlier marriages had all had a ring of adultery to them because they were concise but inexact. For a long time afterward, I still looked in on the women in the supermarkets where they shopped, but we kept out of each other's eyes. I eventually saw every one of them vehemently pregnant—they deployed their bodies to brilliant effect for the men who came after me—and I was always on the verge of sending well-wishing cards with notes attached. But I kept my mind on getting in good with myself and watering down what I wanted from people.

Now I had another wife, and a daughter, to both of whom I was the last person on earth. I have already said everything about the daughter. But the wife, my last one: she was the one I married because how else this late was I going to get an idea of how many things a person did during the course of a day and then make sure I was doing the same number of things—only different ones, to keep me from looking too dependent? I could be civil to this wife once I knew her plans for the day, once I had an inkling of how much work was cut out for me.

Whatever my wife did, I would come up with something collateral, an equivalent. I would keep pace with her—chore for chore, personal occasion for personal occasion.

Except that everything she did fell inside the marriage and everything I did fell anywhere but. I was no good at holding things in. I slid into lavartorial cahoots with strangers. I blabbed everything. Nobody ever got far enough into my mouth to get in the way of what I was saying.

This is where help might have been of some help.

Example: two nights a week my wife volunteered with a program that reached out to people for whom speech had become a hardship. These included the people who said "they" instead of "he" to jack up the population of their private lives. The county college offered a course the same two nights. It did not apply to the source of my livelihood, which shall remain nameless, but I signed up for it and bought the book. A girl sat next to me for weeks before finally markering "How are you fixed for people?" on a page of her thick semestral notebook. She tore out the page, folded it, filliped it toward me.

I wrote back what—that I am people-proof, a onesome?

A story can go on only so long before it stops being a joke.

It was a three-hour class with a fifteen-minute intermission that the prof kept postponing until later and later because no-body but a handful of studious illiterates hung around for what followed it. One night at the start of break the girl pointed out the window at a car that was a black oblong on the parking lot.

In the car, she said, "Guess what I cooked for supper—it stank up my hair."

I sampled a shiny hank of it in my fingers but could not place the smell. She drove me to somebody's house. We stationed our-selves at opposite ends of the living-room floor. When we both saw that that was all there was going to be to it—that just be-cause there is a place for something doesn't automatically mean it belongs there—she drove me back to the lot where my car was.

I told everything to my wife.

Who wouldn't have?

She tracked down the girl by first name alone—called the registrar in one of her voices—and barely made trouble.

I called the girl just once after that.

"I know we had a falling-out," I told her.

I went to grocery stores expecting to find her buying further things to cook.

My teeth started sticking to everything I took bites from.

One morning I could not get out of the house. I tried all of the doors and a couple of the windows. It was as if they were pasted shut. I turned on the radio expecting nothing but static or long lists of school closings, but there was music, music with words rising from it familiarly.

I had to call in sick.

I looked at my wife and daughter. One or the other said something about being hungry for something substantial.

I watched my wife reach into a cabinet for a frying pan. I watched my daughter open the refrigerator door. I duly unloosened myself from my chair. I started off in the direction of the silverware drawer.

I went on with their life. **Q**

Melaleuca

It was the Easter after the rats came and Mama'd made me wear my suit for the whole day after church, even when she sent me walking over to Miss Ruby and them's to borrow Miss Ruby's electric beater because ours only spins at the slow speed and makes a low, humming sound while it does so that Mama thinks it's going to blow up on her. And I had to go over to Pootus's store in my suit too, looking for condensed milk and a bucket of chitterlings so she could make some for Grampa, but Pootus was out of chitterlings and Mama said she wasn't going to worry about it because no matter how much he fusses he don't need to be eating that stuff no ways and she definitely don't need to be smelling up her house cooking them. I sat on the couch and complained about wanting to change my clothes and trying to scratch my feet through my shoes.

"Hush," Mama said. "You can stand looking nice all day for one day out the whole year." But I kept on scratching and complaining. Then she found where the rats had tried to bite through one of the jars we got to keep rice and grits and flour in to keep them from eating it all. She ran water into the lid to see if they'd made a hole in it. I got behind her to try and see too and when I bumped her she yelled for me to get out of her way and quit worrying her. She told me to take the bus to the Grove and bring Grampa back for dinner because we'd be waiting on him all day otherwise, telling me to go straight there and hurry back because she planned to have dinner ready on time and she didn't want Brother Patrick or Miss Ruby and them waiting around to eat.

She didn't have to tell me to hurry up because I didn't want stay gone nowhere in my suit, having to walk all the way to the bus stop with my jacket over my shoulder so I wouldn't sweat to death, my shoes making so much noise against the sidewalks that everybody who wasn't dressed up heard me coming and looked up at me. And everybody else who was dressed up looked as mad as me: mamas who kept getting their high heels caught in cracks and their kids following behind them, pulling at their clothes, all of them sweating so that the girls' pressed bangs were starting to nap and curl up, or if they had plaits the plaits were starting to frizz and come all undone, and greasy little beads of Afro-sheen were dripping out of the boys' hair and onto their collars. Me, I don't need to put nothing in my hair. It doesn't curl up real tight so it can get as long as it wants to and still I can slide a pick or a comb through it as easy as if it was all greased up.

It was a old bus that came, without air-conditioning so that all of the old ladies sitting in front who know Grampa were fanning themselves, looking so tired that the hands they were holding their fans with were flopping around like they weren't attached to their arms while their other hands reached out to me, slowly, shaking some, each one of them grabbing my hand and telling me, "You getting prettier every day, Penny." I smiled at each of them before pulling my hand away from them, doing it slow enough so they wouldn't go and tell Grampa I was being ornery the way Miss Saddler did once and Grampa made me apologize to her in front of my whole Sunday school class. When they was all finished touching on me, I went and sat near the back of the bus just far enough back that I wouldn't have to talk to any them.

It's bad enough having a girl's name without having ladies call me pretty all the time. Nobody calls me by my real name and I don't care if most people call me Penny, just the ladies who think they can turn me into a girl by how they talk to me. Ladies stand behind me and Mama in the grocery store and say, "What a pretty color he is," touching my arm like they expect it's going to rub off on them; like it's something they want to buy for themselves so they can put it on along with all of that yellow and green stuff they like to put on their eyes and all of that orangeish lipstick they outline in black like they making sure everybody knows how big their lips are. Without make-up their lips would just turn into part of their faces at some place you could never really see from far away. I always let Mama tell them thank you and wait for her to slap me on the arm and tell me, "Be polite and thank her," before I say it myself, not looking at who I'm thanking when I say it but at the cash register instead, or a magazine, or the pictures on a box of cake mix that's on the belt, thinking that nobody's ever going to get a cake out the box to look like that, listening to Mama say something about me getting to be a teenager and dancing on her last nerve, and the lady laughing and saying, "Don't I know that's right—I got two myself."

The bus goes out of South Miami and into Coral Gables where it doesn't stop hardly at all. When I ride the bus to school in the mornings, it's full of ladies wearing maid uniforms, the old ladies that sit laughing with each other, chewing tobacco and spitting in a cup and leaning across the aisle to touch each other on the knee and say, "Lord willing, I'll see you tomorrow," before they ring the bell to get off, and the younger, fatter ladies that talk to the driver if he's a brother, leaning against the pole behind his seat while he asks them, "Don't it being hot make you feel like doing it?" and "You best hurry cause massuh's waiting on you," nodding his head at the big car that's parked by the side of the road, running, with some white lady inside that's peeping over the steering wheel at the bus. "Lord, please," the lady'll say and get all her plastic bags together that I can't figure out what all anybody'd keep in them, taking her own sweet time down the steps and down the sidewalk to the white lady's car.

But the day I'm talking about was Easter and the bus was full of nothing but old ladies that was coming back from the big church in Richmond Heights they all go to, all dressed up and quiet, none of them chewing because they was afraid of messing up their dresses, and when these three dudes got on with these two fat-legged white girls and went to stretch out in the last two rows of seats, lighting up a joint when they got there, the girls giggling when they smoked and the brothers looking half-asleep and talking in mumbles I couldn't understand from where I was, all of the old ladies sat up straight in their seats and started trying to whisper to each other, only they so deaf they can't whisper no more. I could hear them saying how the driver should throw them off and how white girls' skin can be so ugly sometimes, what with the way you can see veins and bruises and stuff on it.

"Don't you ever let me catch you back there smoking that stuff," one of them yelled back at me. "I'll knock you out myself and then tell your Mama." I nodded at her and leaned my head against the seat in front of me so she wouldn't see me starting to cry and think I was crying because of her.

It wasn't because of her.

I cry all the time for no reason and always when I'm where folks can see me. I'll be with Dwayne and Doobie and them, listening to Dwayne say, "Miz Marmer best not send me down to Mr. Dilini to get paddled—I'll come to the bitch's house—knock the bitch down and kick her in her pussy, the bitch try and mess with me. Get that foot way up in there too," and he'll stop and say, "What's wrong with you, man? Miz Marmer your girlfriend? The boy's doing her on the side."

I don't even know when I start crying sometimes. I don't feel the tears on my face or won't even be thinking about nothing in particular, just sitting and staring at something. I told everybody it's how I laugh so now I can't laugh at nothing ever. Dwayne'll be walking around, saying, "The bitch walk around like she done sucked somebody up in her pussy, like she grabbed him with that hand she got up in there—that big old hairy hand that's got claws on it and shit—looks like the wolf man's hand or some shit. It reached out of her pussy and grabbed the boy's dick and pulled the boy in." He says that and walks around with his stomach sticking way out, shaking it around like somebody's trying to bust out, saying in a woman's voice, "Don't you worry none, baby— Mama's going to find somebody else to put in there and keep you company," and I can't laugh no matter how much I want to. "Let me see your eyes," he says to me. "I got to see if I'm being funny."

I kept my head down on the seat and listened, drying my eyes enough to look at up at these two girls who live by Grampa when one of them said, "I'm going to come find you when you get old enough to do something for me," and the other one saying, "He could do something for me now," keeping my head down when one of the brothers in back yelled for me to come back and smoke with them. I could hear all the old ladies moving around in their seats, ready to knock me upside the head if I even looked back at them and I heard one of the white girls tell him to leave me alone.

"We just trying to educate the brother," one of them said. "We got a responsibility to make sure he knows what's up." The white girls laughed so hard that they had to spit out the window. And I didn't look up even when the white girls started jumping up in their seats, screaming about seeing a rat poking his head out from under the back seat. I'd never seen one on the bus before, but I don't get surprised about seeing them anywhere no more. I put my legs up on the seat and sat there crying till we got over by where Grampa lives.

Grampa lives in the new building they built for old folks, this tall, gray-looking thing that he hates and that you can't even get into unless somebody knows you're coming and lets you in. "You can't see nothing," he says, "living that far up off the street." He keeps his door open so he can talk to anybody that walks by and keeps his gun in the pocket of his chair just like he did when he lived over by Pootus's, "In case somebody who does come by wants to start something," he says, but hardly anybody walks by his apartment except for Miss Pauline from next door.

They tore down the house where Grampa used to live and all the houses around it. They tore his down last because he didn't want to move. We stood on his porch and watched the bulldozers tear the other houses down, the bulldozers running right into the side of a house so the wall would collapse and the house would start leaning over to one side for second, hanging, until it came off its blocks and it crashed down on the ground or into the house next to it. I watched it with Dwayne and Doobie too, all of us lined up outside the fences they put around blocks of houses they was tearing down. We watched them bulldoze all of the wood and cinder blocks into big pile that the rats would run out of at night.

Grampa didn't know I was coming so I had to knock on the

glass door to get this old lady who was sitting on a chair in the lobby to come and open the door for me. She wasn't doing nothing, but she didn't want to get up. I kept knocking and staring at her till she got up and crept over to the door, opening it just enough for her to stick her nose and mouth out and tell me I needed somebody I knew to let me in. I told her Grampa's name and where he lived and, after acting like she was thinking about it for a while, she opened the door and walked me to the elevator, holding my elbow and telling me to make sure I went straight to Grampa's and not to be messing around in the building because old people's nerves can't take it. When the elevator came, she pushed the button for the fifth floor for me and watched me while the doors was closing. When they was all the way closed, I pushed the buttons for three and four and six, just because I knew she was still down there, watching to see if I went where I was supposed to. I like messing with people when I know I ain't doing nothing wrong.

Grampa was asleep in his chair with the TV on to some white man pointing up to God and talking without moving his head. Grampa's apartment's almost empty, with nothing in the living room but his chair and his TV and the TV tray he eats off. He wouldn't move his stuff out of his house before they tore it down. "What I need with stuff when I ain't got no real place to put it?" he said. Me and Mama went and got his clothes and some other stuff for him, Mama saying the whole time she had half a mind to leave the TV and the chair because it'd serve him right not having no place to sit and nothing to do all day. But she got Mr. Macon to put the chair and TV and the bed in his van and bring it down here and Mama took all the pictures that was stuffed in his drawers and sitting loose between the pages of his picture albums and put them into new albums for him that he keeps stacked on the floor in the corner. Mama bought silver frames to put other pictures in, pictures of me and Mama together, and of my grandma who I never met and of Grampa's wife who I only remember because I went to her funeral. She put them on the dresser in his bedroom and I go in to sneak looks at the picture of my grandma, sneaking because Grampa grunts and looks at me funny if he sees me looking at her. He has to be in the right mood to talk about her. She's young in the picture, with her hair all long and straight and black and even in black and white I can almost see how she was the same rust color as me.

I shook Grampa for a while before he woke up and, when he did wake up, he wasn't startled or nothing. He opened his eyes halfway and smiled. "You need you another dollar?" he asked me. He pulled a big roll of dollars out of his shirt pocket and tried to get hold of one of them, but he dropped them all down on his lap.

"I don't need no dollar," I said. I said, "Come on, we got to get to the house for dinner." But he was still messing with the dollars, trying to get them back together. I tried to help him, but he slapped me on the arm when I did.

"You stay away from my money till I shut my eyes," he said. "Then you can take what you want to. But I'm still alive and it's my damn money." Being angry got him waked up some and he sat up and concentrated. He rubbed all the dollars on his knee to get them flat and put them on the arm of the chair. There was sixteen of them and, when he got them all stacked and facing in the same direction, he folded them over once and pulled one out and gave it to me.

"Don't ask me for more," he said.

"We got to go for dinner," I said.

But we both sat there for a long while, me looking at his fingers, trying to imagine what they could of looked like when he was young, and him just staring until he got up and walked to the door without saying nothing.

He was quiet on the bus, just waving at the people he knows but not saying nothing to them. And he dozed some, leaning his head back and snoring. But when we got back to South Miami, he was awake and started walking to Pootus's instead of going to the house, and I didn't say nothing to him, not really wanting to go walking around in my suit but not wanting to try and tell him about Mama waiting with dinner either because I knew he wouldn't listen. Doobie says that's how come they let me hang around them even though I ain't in junior high yet—because I know when to shut up. I tied the sleeves of my jacket around my neck so I wouldn't have to hold it no more and followed him to Pootus's store.

Pootus was leaned up against the coolers when we came in, saying, "What it is, old man?" soon as he saw us. Pootus opened the cooler door and watched Grampa get his can of Ballantine and the bottle of Nehi for me and walked to the counter two steps in front of us, his high-water pants that are always too tight showing how skinny he is—skinnier than you'd think anybody who can hold three cases of beer over his head with one hand could be—not resting the cases on the flat part of his hand but balancing them on his fingertips, his other hand in his pocket and a cigarette between his lips that he smokes slowly without ever looking like he's losing his breath. His face is all angular and shiny black, "black as my shoe," Mama says. I could look at him forever if it wasn't that somebody'd think I was turning faggot on them.

Grampa gave him the money and left without saying good-bye or nothing and Pootus winked at me when I waved bye to him. We went down the street to where the Cuban man sells pork chop sandwiches out of the old ice cream truck. When Grampa used to live around here, he ate them every day and I ate them with him every time I could. Mama used to tell me not to go with him because only niggers who ain't got enough sense to fry their own pork chops and put them on white bread theyselves would line up to pay somebody to do it for them. "Folks like that," she said, "don't know how to do nothing but spend all their money so they can keep on being niggers like they always been." But Grampa says the Cuban man has a special spice and can't Mama or nobody else make a sandwich taste like that. Me, I like the white paper they come in, with big warm spots of grease all on the outside. I peel it off a little bit at a time and let the steam get all on my lips and up my nose.

The Cuban man was telling Grampa, "I was going to have to close without you coming," while Grampa was counting out the four dollars to pay him, dropping one on the ground twice so I had to pick it up. We went back over to the vacant lot behind Pootus's where Mr. Mac and Mr. N. was sitting, each of them with they own beer and Mr. Mac with a pork chop bone that he'd scraped all the meat off of and was trying to suck the marrow out of one end. They were arguing about the Cuban mayor, Mr. N. saying it was his fault they tore down all the old houses around here, "so he could put more black folks out on the street," Mr. N. said. "He don't care about me. He just wants to make it so more of them can come over here and get them someplace to live." But Mr. Mac was saying that it weren't none of the mayor's fault Mr. N.'s house was going to fall down on top of him. Mr. Mac said even if the mayor is putting black folks out on the street, it's as many of us as it is of them, and it's black folks' fault we ain't got ourselves together enough to get our own mayor. Mr. Mac said, "Black folks are too busy killing each other to get theyselves together," he said, "and I ain't going to be sorry about nobody that ain't taking responsibility for theyself."

Me and Grampa sat down and Grampa was nodding his head and saying, "You damn right," at what both of them was saying, and letting little clumps of bread fall out onto his lips.

Mr. Mac said, "That boy the police killed didn't take no responsibility for hisself and I ain't going to feel sorry for him neither. Any of them little niggers you see around here all doped up and half-crazy could get themselves shot the same way he did and shouldn't you or nobody else feel sorry for them when they do. That's what I say and I just said it."

I knew the boy he was talking about, the one that got shot. He was always asking me for money even though I never had none to give to him. He never looked at me when he put his hand out, his arms all full of sores and trash and stuff all in his hair from where he was sleeping on the ground. He just looked off down the street and said, "C'mon and help a brother out," and "You smoke that reefer, right? Well, I know where you can get you some." He was older than me but not taller. I can't see how he thought he could of beat a policeman up.

"It's all this dope that's messing black folks up," Mr. Mac said. But he don't mean reefer. I've seen Mr. Mac smoking that himself, sitting on the front porch of his house with his head bent down, his neck getting all tight from sucking so hard. But all dope's the same to Mama and Miss Ruby. We drive past the high school where the boys smoke right next to the street, holding their joints up like they offering it to everybody who's passing by, and Mama and Miss Ruby say, "Lord help us when y'all got to go to school there," Mama touching the wooden cross that hangs from her mirror and Miss Ruby starting to mumble her prayers like she does anytime anything happens, even if she drops a fork. I never smoked none myself because I know somebody'd see me if I did and I can't even think about how mad Mama'd get if she found out.

"Black folks is too busy killing each other for dope that they ain't got time to do nothing else," Mr. Mac was saying.

"You right about that," Mr. N. said, "but you get you a white boy on dope and a black boy on dope and you see who the policeman decides to shoot first. That's what I'm talking about."

Mr. Mac said, "But it's stuff in the air too that's making people act crazy like they do. If your air and water ain't good, you get sick, not just your body but your head too. That's where all this foolishness is coming from."

Mr Mac was always saying how it's stuff from the war—all the smoke and noise and the burning rubber and metal all in his throat that made it so his legs don't work no more. They went on talking like that, Mr. N. saying how Mr. Mac don't know nothing about reality no more from living up in his big house with wheelchair ramps all in it. "The Lord's going to take what use I got left in my legs away from me for Christmas," Mr. Mac says. "I'm just getting ready. It's going to be his present to me, not having to worry about them no more." Mr. Mac said the same thing last year, but Christmas came and went and he's still walking the same, just complaining about it more.

Grampa said how he wished he'd of been in the war so he could of got him some money too.

"You too foolish," Mr. Mac said. "You'd of never gotten back with a ass to hold up your pants with."

I half listened, waiting for stuff I like to hear, like how Mr. Mac had other soldiers spitting on him, and, if Grampa's talking, about how he helped build the wall that runs behind our house and all the other houses on our side of the block. I listened and thought about the sores on my arms from mosquito bites. I used to think it was the white part of me showing through, just like the big white patches that's all over Mama's neck, only mine are smaller because I'm less white than she is. I thought if I kept getting bites and kept picking at them, I'd turn white all over. But I don't want to turn white anymore and, besides, the white patches don't stay. They darken up and disappear. I was looking at my skin, saying my name over and over in my head and thinking I wasn't pretty at all.

Grampa stood up to dig around in his pocket for his money and told me to go in and get him another beer and another soda for myself if I wanted it. When I was just a couple of steps away, Mr. N. leaned over and tried to whisper to Grampa that he'd seen my Daddy driving around just up the road. But they can't whisper no more either. So I probably could of heard it even if I'd been inside Pootus's. I turned my head some to see them because you can't hardly believe something somebody's saying if you don't see them saying it. I saw Mr. N. leaned forward in his chair and Grampa standing up, bent over at the waist to put his ear next to Mr. N.'s mouth. They was both looking right at me and when they saw I was looking at them, Mr. N. sat up in his chair and Grampa tried to stand up straight, to look like he was trying to stick his dollars back in his pocket. But he lost his balance. When he stepped back to catch himself, his foot hit the chair and he fell backwards.

I rode to the hospital in the ambulance with him and told the doctors at the hospital how old he was and that I only saw him drink one beer and what our number was so they could call Mama. He didn't get hurt bad, but they didn't tell Mama that when they called her. She ran in the hospital with her shoes in her hand and I could tell she was crying even before I could see her face. She wouldn't listen to me tell her he was all right. She wanted to see the doctor herself and when he came out, he held his hands up to her shoulders like he was going to touch her to make her feel better. But he didn't touch her. He kept his hands there for a while until he told her Grampa didn't have nothing but a big cut and he only passed out because he was old and drunk. Then she wasn't crying no more but she was still all upset.

They brought Grampa out to the where we was in a wheelchair with the back of his head shaved and bandaged up and him smiling and looking silly when he saw us. Mama started getting on him for being drunk and foolish on the Lord's day, but saying it all softly like if you heard it from another room and couldn't understand the words you'd imagine that she was hugging him. She pushed him out to where the car was and helped him get in it herself, whispering to him, "Take it easy now, we ain't in no rush," and him telling her back that he was fine, to let him alone.

When we was all in the car she asked him, "You hungry?"

"I'm always hungry," Grampa said. He looked out of the window and started humming.

"I was born hungry and I'll die hungry," Grampa said, and went back to humming.

Shit, I loved that old man. **Q**

My Little Pledge of Us

We were Russia.

We weren't only Russia. We were Bessarabia, which meant we included those small cities and towns, Galatz and Reni, just across the River Prut in Roumania. Our grandfather was Egypt. Our mother's papers said Persia. There were months in Constantinople. Our great-grandfather Soltanitzky, the composer to the Sultan. There were certain Belgians. A Polish-Mexican arrived and said he was our uncle.

So much of this happened in another language.

In the easy suburban evening our parents waited for our American disaster. We were schooled in the talk of fires. We knew what should be grabbed. We were taught to recognize the men who would one day walk up our front walk to take candlesticks, a bribe. We knew the smell of gypsies who would come to take the youngest child.

In our house everything ran too hot or too cold.

But don't get me wrong. We girls were girls who could ride bikes. We girls ate franks, had TV dinners on Sunday nights.

So, of course, please, don't worry, come in.

Come in out of the barbecue evening, step over the potsys marking the hopscotch game, out of range of the bells of the Good Humor truck. Come in through the red curtain to here where it smells of cooked beets and sour cream, of sorrel and koulibiak. Come in where the vodka is in cups. Don't be shy. We have no time, only generations. Raise a finger, a voice. Chime in. Everyone is speaking, all at once, all in different languages.

Please to the table, of course you will eat.

A spinach pie.

A blintz.

A cabbage soup.

Sha sha.

Speak up. Have more. Have more. Have a spoon or three of the caviar Mattus has smuggled in the bellies of painted nesting dolls. Squish in, among the dead and the living and the children.

Introductions?

That can all come later.

Now it is enough to know that they came with our faces on them. Out of waters, off of boats, onto wharf and land, they came with our long and with our skinny faces, only longer and skinnier, and when they spoke through our bulbed lips, and did not speak our tongue, we shook our heads to say we understood.

Such tales.

So it is said that our great-grandfather knelt on one knee and played a melody so sweet that the Sultan leaned over and kissed our great-grandfather's head.

So it is said that our mother learned to dance her tarantella from a strumming band of wine soaked merchants.

So it is said.

It is said and it is said and we girls said *Cithagan yithagou ith-agundithagerstithagand mithagee*?

Natured, nurtured, everyone at this table has a fantastic, tortured story.

How will it be told? With a needle and a spoon it will be told. And it will be told, too, with a mother's waltz and a father's worry coin and with a treasure box where the youngest child has hidden buttons and feathers, the woolly scraps that help her to sleep, the soup spoon and bread crust she will need when the gypsies steal her and she must find her way back home. It will be told secretly, camouflaged, in a mended language made newly of the old frayed words. It will be spoken in tarnished silver, in a beaten egg and a whisper, and in the shouting all at once voices of all the relatives each claiming the other is dreaming, has it wrong and that his story, her story, this story is the only story, the one to ward off disaster, the only one that is right.

Ah, gypsies.

Ah, Galatz.

Have a little more herring, no?

Behind our house were the woods we called the River Prut, where we girls ran to hide, drifting on layers of damp rotting leaves, floating over to the edge of the woods to see whether our house was in flames yet or if the milkman had dragged our mother off in his metal truck.

Was there ever a disaster? Was there ever a time that we were actually called to the front, we three girls, their young recruits, we three girls, already defectors, armed and trained to shoot to kill? If it had come to killing, what would we have killed? A cossack? A postman? The slow boy who lived down the block? Our mother? Our father?

In the woody River Prut we stashed away rations that we claimed would hold us for a week. We worked our way through a box of crackers in an afternoon and buried the empty carton. My sister said we would learn to survive on air. She gave us each one of Mama's cigarettes. We foraged for acorns. We chewed sticks. We made plans for a rendezvous at the mouth where the River Prut meets the Danube.

We were, always, finally, their only disaster. There was our mother standing at the back door screaming our names. Bloody noses. A stitched eye. Our papa waiting up for us when we tottered in, smokey, from parties we swore were chaperoned. We were always teetering, on the verge of looking too much like whatever was out there.

"You are not American," our father said when we marched with the school band.

"You are not American," our father said when a sister came downstairs frosted-lipped, wearing a black arm band.

"What do you think you are?" our father asked. For enough of the time we girls were like everybody else, kids hanging from trees, kids with forks and stiff-legged dolls, kids looking for other kids we could tease for being different or dumb, some kid my sister tricked into eating soap powder, the slow boy we bribed to strip almost naked, anyone we could master or make stick out so that we did not stick out quite as much.

From the banks of the River Prut we watched our house. We saw how our family must look to the others on our street. What was inside looked suspicious, our uncle in shirtsleeves waving a wooden spoon, our mother and father rushing at each other, playing bullfight with a table spread. We could hear our father shouting, "Do you think I am the Tzar." It was not what our father said but how he said it, his rhythm all wrong, and the way he switched mid-sentence into another of his languages or stopped at a window and stared out as if he were seeing our street for the first time.

Mostly though, even in daytime, the shades of our house were drawn. They were foreign inside, shadows stretched funny by light and we could not recognize exactly who was who or what lived inside of that house.

We could see our mother, the strained look on her face when she called, "Girls." She stood in the doorway in a sheer wrap skirt and tights. "Girls," she repeated, getting softer with a fear we could watch overtake her body so that soon she was not so much walking through our yard as she was creeping through it, whispering our names.

"Don't go back!" our sister said.

"Girls," our mother trembled close to us. Our oldest sister grabbed our wrists.

"Don't even breathe," our sister said.

We thought about the air we had eaten. It should hold us. We pretended our mother was not our mother. It burned where our sister's nails dug into our skin.

"Please," our mother whispered, bargaining with the soldiers we knew she believed had come for us.

It looked terrible—our mother hunching through the yard in her chiffon skirt. She stumbled and muttered. The ground was muddy with spring. We could have touched her, come out to her or brought her into our hideout on the banks of the River Prut. We let her stay out there, wheeling and crawling through the yard, calling out for her children until doors opened. Other parents cradling babies, a hand protectively on the neck of the older ones, came out for a look.

Our mother ran in for our father. Our oldest sister said she deserved the worry, the way our mother dressed in slippers that laced at her ankles. Our sister asked did we see any other mother who drove through town in leotards, a camel-hair jacket draped over her shoulders?

Our oldest sister started singing. "Oh beautiful," she sang. She walked up to the front door singing. We followed. "For purple mountains," we sang together. Our parents came to the door. Our father said something to our mother in a language we did not understand. She pulled in, standing close to him. They looked past us to the other neighbors watching our family from their front steps.

"Are you through?" our father asked, though it sounded to us like *true*.

The wind was thick behind us, racketing in over the woody River Prut.

"Come in, girls," our mother said, flaring her nostrils once. We went in.

The bowls of kasha were still burning hot.

Now is the time.

It might as well be the time, I think, to relax, get cozy, take off the shoes if you have not already, and make our introductions. Mama, the mother; Papa, the father; Nana Gusta with her sisters and her brothers, and her husband, our grandfather, and his father and perhaps, too, the drunk Sultan himself with his thirst for music, and Uncle Marie with his good head of hair and his sour wives and their curdled offspring, and even here, too, is Fokine, nephew of the famous Mr. Fokine and Madame Swoboda, and Esperanza, one of the Flamenco twins from Seville, and Irina Fedovata and the Polish uncle from Mexico that we called Monsieur Max.

Shake hands.

Kiss cheeks—both cheeks.

Do not you worry that you cannot remember the one from the other. Stay a little while, have a bowl of Fokine's bouillabaisse, and you will start somehow to simmer in dialects of languages that you have never learned. There are, of course, others—a cousin who arrived by mail, floated in when my parents forgot themselves and left a door slightly ajar. There were cakes named for aunts who never showed up and there was an extra sister we believed our mother kept in the old bassinet just in case the youngest child never found her way back home.

Us girls? We are the daughters one, two, and four, the third our mother's fifth-month loss. We are called for always all at once. We come downstairs together, a flock, flutter and hem, hand-me-downs handed down twice. We are the Anderson sisters, shoulder to shoulder to shoulder singing, "Daisy, Daisy answer my question true." Myrna, Louise, Greta, Bette, and Marilyn, we name ourselves straight out of Hollywood. Our names change with the marquee each week.

Seen but not heard, napkins bunchy with bread and lox, we are off to resupply our stash on the River Prut.

We will be back.

In the meantime, try the pirogi?

Our mother rode through town in her tights and chiffon wrap skirt, a camel-hair jacket draped over her shoulders, the pink slippers ribboned to her feet. Rumor was she had danced with the Bolshoi and for a season with the Ballet Russe de Monte Carlo.

"That girl—not one but three left feet." Mama laughed, and flicked cigarettes onto trim lawns.

The town police waited for our mother. They liked to pull her over, stand at the window and ask her to step outside, "for just a moment, please." Our mother went Frenchie on us for the town police, everything Z-ish and high rolling R's, her chiffon dance skirt melting in the headlights. She had a kick to her, up on tip toes, arched and ready for a can-can. We watched the policeman light a cigarette for our mother. She dipped, swayed, gave a little curtsy. We saw the taut line between her shoulders, her readiness to take off and run. They took their time each time—warnings, radio checks, rules explained so slowly so that when our mother got back in the car she said, "All the same, those guards, *les idiots*. Take me home, girls," and she would pull off, smoking out just a bit too fast.

The Russians had nothing good to say about one another. They were always fighting, our Mother and Fokine, about shrimp or Fokine's famous uncle Mr. Fokine or our electric stove which Fokine said was impossible and made true bouillabaisse impossible or our mother saying what did an old Russian know from bouillabaisse having never been anywhere closer to Marseille then a bowl of borscht.

The house smelled fishy. Bass heads glanced up out of pots. There were legs on the counter. Grunt and eel leaned, scaled and clean, on the cutting board.

And there were always other Russians in our kitchen saying other no good things to one another. There were sudden bursts of silence. They watched each other with slandering eyes.

The kitchen reeked of garlic.

In our house there was no grace. There were split shells on the table. There was wine. There was Fokine polishing over our polish. There were more fights among the Russians. There was a mazurka and a polonaise. There was rum. There were cries of *Bolshevik*. There were stains on the linen. There was an aria from Monsieur Max, who fell in love with Esperanza, the elder flamenco twin from Seville. There was the youngest child napping in our papa's lap, waking up enough to say, "I am not sleepy." There were dishes in the sink and dishes on the table and an open bottle of cognac and our papa carrying us one by one up to our beds to tuck us—God willing—in for the night.

Outside, at intersections, with their oaths and eager badges, we were certain they waited.

They would wait all night if they had to.

They would pledge themselves ready for what they knew

had already crossed the border, had infiltrated, assimilated, weakened the dollar.

They would wait in the dark till it came.

They would flip a switch, pin it in spotlight.

They would cruise the streets of our town listening to the electric wires.

They would get out the dogs.

They would make it walk the yellow line.

They would watch for lapses.

They would look it in the eye, warn it, ticket it.

They would dismantle it.

They would make it hoist the flag.

They would keep it out.

They would wait all night to keep it out.

They would maintain the order.

Inside in our house, the Sultan, glutted, exhausted, arbitrary as ever, kissed each of our travelled foreheads, closed his one good eye, and, for at least this night, kept the assassins out.

Monsieur Max sat outside on a plastic lawn chaise and waited for the Mexican wind that he said passed through our woods.

"That's my Oaxaca, girls," said our uncle, closing his eyes.

We sat behind him at the edge of the woods. Monsieur Max said that out of the woods was coming the Mexican Wind and up the street was coming the Armies of Europe.

It was gummy in our yard, the road filmy with heat.

"Oh, yes," said Max. "Here it comes, girls."

We closed our eyes most of the way, kept him a flickery thing, a bulge and sag in the grass.

We could hear kids down the street. They were a motley after-dinner band, brothers straggling behind brothers, sisters, any kid who wasn't inside or off anywhere better, wandering to the corner, looking for other kids who had wandered out, stringing together chase or war or red rover red rover or just sitting on the curb waiting for another kid who might have an idea.

Monsieur Max said there were bandits in these woods, and that, fierce and cruel as a Mexican bandit was, we should hide under their wool serapes when the Armies of Europe landed on our street. "Among enemies," our uncle said, "choose your friends."

We could hear them down the street. We could hear that the teams were uneven.

It blued with shadow by the woods where we sat behind Monsieur Max.

"Under their serapes there is always something—a tortilla, a chipped knife, an bottle to fill with wind for when they flee their country," he said.

He stood up to turn his chair and sat back down.

"Remember, a bandit," our uncle said, "is not so different— like a Polish soldier—that same hollow knock."

He stood up to turn his chair and sat back down.

The game was growing, we could hear it, a mailbox base for safety, someone screaming, "That's not fair," screaming, "Yes," screaming and screaming and screaming until that was, we knew, the game—kids screaming out of bushes, through flower beds, tagging and bombing, tagged and bombed, and now we could hear the mothers out screaming, "Right now!" and "Your father!" and "I mean it!" until they were gone and the street was so quiet with quiet and dark with the first dark of night.

Monsieur Max said, "There it is, my Valladolid."

We thought we felt it then, the wind, whatever, something in that heat that came through us.

We shut our eyes and waited for more.

"You are not American," our father said.

He said it, it seemed to us, the way we heard other fathers tell their children not to run out into the street. He said it to us as if the worst had already happened, the way we knew those other fathers knew that there is always a child lurching after a stray ball and getting hit.

Papa called us in from evening street games to look at

our books. "All wrong," he said. It was, we said, the way they wanted it done.

There was, Papa said, the problem of the numbers. There was the problem of the straightness of rows. There was, our father said, the entire problem of American teachers that were, he said, hardly teaching anything but a poorness of all habit that might prove to be needed.

We loved them one and all, our teachers with their crisp blouses and blue grade books. Oh, to her blond flip, and after Christmas the diamond ring that Miss Skilken held up to the light. We loved the nurse's cot where we rolled the thermometer under our tongue. Oh, to color-coded readers, stories of girls and boys out on picnics, the mother with her pleated skirt at the open door. We loved the shop teacher with his jigsaw and belt sander and Mrs. Herman who read us the news and cried for the hungry children on the other side of the world.

"It will be needed," Papa said. Our father paced the floor, his money belt strapped under his shirt. "And what is all this?" he asked, waving our compositions.

Oh, too, to the under-desk minutes where we practiced waiting for the Russian bomb. Our father said the teachers listened— a giveaway vowel, a lapse into any language. We were the Russias. Any explosion was ours. We were tongue-tied, students of the way our teachers spoke, a Boston *r* we brought home, announcing at the table, "Miss Brenner says that's not true." Papa saying with his sharp look, "I'll show you true."

"All too much," he said, "and too much against America." He blew into the backs of his fingers. "So much opinion? Who are you? The President?" He jiggled his belt, feeling for coins that would pay his way across borders, buy us a new name. We rewrote our compositions while he blew hard into his fingers again to keep —despite his squandered, lost children—what little he had hoarded of luck.

But too much talk without nothing! Not so much this as a blintz or a kugel. Not a nothing little sweet? Not a little burek stuffed with spinach and sweet cheese. Not even a tea, the leaves at the bottom forever spelling out doom.

Come, come with us. We will sneak away from the table, down the stairs to the basement where the costumes Nana sews for Mama's ballet are kept.

There are Chinese courtesans, snowflakes, brocade dresses for Cinderella's nasty sisters, bolts of toile and crepe, sequins tacked and stacks of crowns, garlands, the Sugarplum Fairy's tutu, a tutu for each season hung upside down on hangers from the pipes in our basement where we girls went to light matches and smoke our mother's cigarettes.

Our hands were our mother's hands, her cigarettes put to our mouths, or held ashy at a distance until the ashes dropped. The ashes always dropped. Our legs were ashy and seared where we tested each other, burning the faint hairs down to skin. Our skin was our mother's skin, traversed, foreign, each of us girls a country she crept through to come to bring us forth.

We could hear them through the ceiling and in the pipes, our father counting his stacks of coins, making money belts for each of us, planning and replanning routes out of town, towns to go to, countries where someone else was already living with our name. We could hear Mother opening the back door, asking Father, "Where are the girls?" We were right there below them, lighting books of matches. They were never out of sound, the scuffle of feet above us mapping their worries. Their feet seemed slow to us. These were the easy feet to catch, walking predictable turns through rooms, heavy feet, easy to catch up with or run from. We were getting ready to make the run. We stuck matches together, watched them fuse and burn out. We burned our nails and the soles of our feet. We put on the wolf's costume and consumed the swan. We put on the swan's costume and never became the prince's bride. We blew smoke rings in the crotch of Sleeping Beauty. We woke as Sleeping Beauty, torched the castle, and went back to sleep. We woke into the fifteenth century in the burning city of Bern, filled our wooden buckets and prayed.

We woke in our basement in our house on our same street to

the smell of tart apple and brandy and brown sugar in the skillet. We woke tired and weak of foot.

There was crème fraîche on the table.

Spoons in every bowl.

We hurried to eat more than our share.

The River Prut flooded. Leaves covered our yard. Our father said, "Look at us." We looked almost like every other American family out for Saturday chores, raking, piling leaves to burn. We were all out, even Fokine in his grey suit picking leaves one by one. Mother called out orders. We were to get under the rose bushes and up on the rose bushes where leaves had spun up and stuck on the thorns. The thorns made our hands bleedy and we wiped the blood on the legs of our pants. Monsieur Max stood up from his plastic lawn chair and called out to the brutal winds of Chiapas that he said tore through our woods. It was, declared Monsieur Max, like the love he loved for Esperanza, something to make a man sing. We heard our father singing songs in languages with notes we could not imitate. "Only in America," said our father. The piles of leaves toppled and fell and we girls fell too, our parents scattering, falling after us, trying to save us from drowning in the River Prut.

We offer our youngest sister for a look at the slow boy scrawling her name with his dick piss. We will double with Dutch for titty for his father's cigarettes, and more too about where our parents have buried arms and the thing we swear to him we have seen a bandit do to a boy with his bandit teeth. We could, it feels, keep talking, and we do, telling the boy how to say *fuck* in Pogo Pogo, how we have seen a man charm a snake down his throat, how our uncle has killed a soldier just with words. The eldest is our talker, walking around the slow boy in fast circles until, grinding and turning after her, he stumbles against the road curb. We take him roughly. We speak in Crocodile and Bulgarian. She tells the slow boy that there are places for a boy like him. "Just look!" she points at his wadded pants. "You're dead." We leave him, scraped, road pebbles stuck bloody to his knees. We leave him with his pants down.

We walk home.

We are spies and counterspies.

We are starlets hiding bombs in the spangle of dresses.

They are hiding out in that house waiting for the soldier and the milkman with his metal truck.

We are running.

Here we come.

Listen . . . you can hear the Sultan's dreams when he takes his night sleep by day at our dinner table. The Sultan always sleeps by day, fighting Turks in his empire. He tosses, wipes tears from his one good eye on our tablecloth, rises crusty-eyed and hungry when we are called to eat.

Watch . . . he will not eat from his own plate, not with a fork or with his hands, not until we are all done and the plates are bones and chewed stems and the cabbage we girls spread to the china's far rim. Not until then and then some. The Sultan starts with our mother's plate, sucking at the blued empty shells she has stacked, using an end of bread to sop up juice of spinach and garlic from our father's plate and over our plates he winks at us, his mouth stuffed full now of all that we girls have wasted.

We were always, he said, in the Sultan's dreams, wielding great swords. We were true armsmen, beheading without a second thought when the Sultan cried out for a head. The Sultan said we showed our family's refined taste, catching with a free, gloved hand and never letting a head just drop.

But to listen into his dreams we let his empires fall.

What burned by whose hand where? What woods are these? The scorched pot? The soup all gone? Where stirred the wind? The Prut, we girls knew, the Danube turned and running inland? A bag of shells? A cigarette? The polished gleam off Fokine's shoes? The tutus aflame? The flames flared out the window like a red flag? What did they see?—the slow boy standing on Monsieur Max's lawn chair screaming *fuck* in Pogo Pogo, the fathers in a huddle behind him? Did they come in the night or by day the milkman in his metal truck? Did they ride off with the pretty sister whooping, "Take me!"? Or with the prettier sisters did they kiss and steal into the woods? Whose woods? I think I know. Every house became a secret language. Everything on fire. But nothing burned.

The Sultan sighed in his sleep. He called out for us in the names he had for us and you could hear in the pause between his cries that we girls, his darlings, were traitors, ministering to him so tenderly from a poisoned cup.

We had no accent.

Every language they spoke in that house was a secret language, a code we were always on the verge of breaking.

We spoke English.

We have walked into rooms into far cities and felt at home in the cluck and warble of what we could not understand. We understand so little. What we do not understand pulses, clots familiarly inside. A worried thread we pull. The frayed, woolly edge of a child's blanket. We have had our children. We have wandered into Russian beauty shops and under the facialist's puffy hands and gossip's tongue fallen fast asleep. We wake to the fighting of Romanian cocks. We feel a wind and hear it's Mexican heat.

Our sister sleeps in a pinstriped suit.

Our sister has the messy scrawl of a poet.

Our sister is a mother.

We wake into the disaster of another calm day.

We wake again.

She wakes from a dream of her father who is not sleeping. He walks in her dream through the halls, stopping at doorways, counting heads. She takes her money belt down to the market and buys her future long. She finds her daughter squatting over a mirror trying to see up to her heart.

Today is the Fourth of July.

Please come to our houses. We will feed you, a little something, a glass of pale wine. Our doors, we leave them open. We douse charcoal with lighter fluid. We light matches. We have no accents. We eat burgers with catsup, dogs with mustard.

We hear of fleeing, the ones who come on boats.

What a pack of liars is this Russia!

Do you think our father saved a single one?

We gather with the others to watch fireworks.

One sister writes, "It is the Fourth of July." One sister holds her son in her lap. He says, "Boom." One sister watches for interest rates to plunge.

They are gone, Monsieur Max and our mother's chiffon skirt.

The money belts are tied up in treasury bills and bonds.

It is America. We are America. We have no accents.

The house is a house that looks like every other house, the River Prut a straggly tangle of trees, our mama, our papa—just someone's mother and father we watch age into the common fretting of the old.

Cithagan yithagou ithagundithagerstithagand mithagee?

My sisters say I have it all wrong. I leave out what is important.

We speak such good English.

I leave out Amelia Wanderling and Paul Logaurcia, who dances the part of the prince. I have not said enough about Uncle Marcie's good head of hair. Have I said containment? Have I said how we held our hands to our hearts and pledged ourselves? How we are sisters who let nothing burn?

There are seconds on burgers, if you are still hungry.

We live, all of us, in the same city, on the same bus line, close to the freeway. We read with a tribal heart about cities in ruin.

They say there are no gypsies.

I have not said Akerman.

The band starts to play. The crowd cheers.

See? The Sultan closes his one good eye when the band starts to play. He listens. The Sultan drifts, with a wheeze and a God bless America, into dreamless sleep.

My sisters say there is no Sultan.

Drink up. It is the Fourth of July. This is my America.

I have got it all wrong. **Q**

The Meditation

I was thinking about some money.

Seemed like I had some coming to me, a lump sum, but I could not for the life of me think of where it might be coming from.

A suitcase full of cash.

A metal suitcase like in the movies. Like you saw business-men carrying out at the airport.

Money aside, I had always admired those suitcases. I didn't travel much, but if I ever travel again, I would like to go with a metal suitcase. Take the tough treatment and look good—that must be the advantage.

Meanwhile, my buddy Steve was talking.

—I'm driving to work on the freeway, early, early this morning. It's barely light, doing maybe seventy.

—Yeah.

—Maybe seventy-five, but I'm careful because, you know, it's freezing and on the overpass—

—Bridge may ice, I said.

—I'm going under a bridge. I watch like a sentry; there's a kid going across slow. Sometimes they drop rocks or cinder blocks.

—Thank God they aren't dropping dynamite.

—Kid didn't drop anything. I look over at the ditch, and there's a dead cat on the lip of a culvert.

I shook my head.

—I see geese, sometimes, flocks of them flying out your way.

Guy down the bar from our table piped in. Older guy, maybe fifty-five or sixty, but pretty well preserved.

—You think that's something, he said. I watch everything—ditch, bridge, bushes. It's hell.

—Don't look, I said.

—Gets to you, guy said, all that watching. You don't want to get yourself into that. Starts out innocent enough, but you do it all the time, it gets habitual.

—That's it, habitual, Steve said.

—Takes a better man than me by far, guy said.

—They're gonna get you anyway, Steve said. Get inside you one way or the other. They want to know how you're wired.

—I've been thinking, I said.

—They don't need to know what you think. Not now, Steve said. Not anymore.

—Hey, I've been thinking, I said. **Q**

Blood Melon

In the lake on a raft, they floated. The girl kicking, splashing, so much that everybody else in the frothy water stayed clear of them, left the water when they saw the raft inflating on the beach—the mother's head disappearing behind it. The girl appeared to like water.

Her mouth was open.

The raft was yellow.

I am just saying it might have been then, when the mother and the girl were on the yellow raft, floating, the girl in that checked bathing suit that must have belonged to the mother, the mother mouthing, "Isn't this nice?" over and over until I knew that nothing at all was ever nice. It would have been then, with a handful of pebbles or maybe some collected stones, the smooth ones I kept in a styrofoam cup, the kind I took home with me from the foot of our lake.

The mother took the girl with her everywhere.

On the sand in a beach chair, the mother sat the girl up and crossed the girl's legs, which I saw were overgrown with hair but not unshapely, not an unshapely pair of legs at all. And breasts. Well, in that bathing suit, probably padded—but pointy.

Did I tell you hair? Black and foresting, under her arms and all over her legs and coming out from the bottom of her bathing suit. You would think that the mother could have done the girl a small favor, just the tiniest little favor, and shaved the hair off the girl with a razor which would not have been so much to ask. The mother held the girl's hands in her hands which might have been to stop the girl from waving her arms around the way she did or might have been to keep the girl's hands from finding their way into the bottom of her bathing suit which they som times did. Or the mother might have held the girl's hands in her hands because it made the mother feel safe, somehow.

This was the summer I learned that bunnies breathe through their ears. I was the same age as the girl, the age you would come home with a five-dollar bunny from the county fair. The age your mother might first allow you to go to the county fair without her.

On a dusty white bike the mother rode the girl in a special seat behind her. The mother even took the girl with her to mah-jongg. Propped the girl up at the corner of the card table with the ladies going at it, clicking their fuchsia nails against the tiles, winning the savings out of each other's change purses or cookie jars and forking into angel food cake, saying, "I really shouldn't!" and ignoring the girl. (They were mothers, you know.)

I don't think they could look.

Of course, neither could I. Or what it was was that I couldn't stop looking, but always only sideways and I saw the mother see this, my looking sideways at her girl.

Did you ever see how a bunny's ears are—so pink and right? Those little tributaries in breathless blues running throughout. Delicate and luxurious also how they stand up so straight like that on end without any help at all. (You can almost understand the dog's irritation until you remember the bunny's gasping.)

One of the ladies explained this to me about bunnies.

"Suffocation, like with a plastic bag, do you know what I mean?" she said. This was unfathomable but somewhat dismissable because this suntanned lady had no breasts at all and a husband with green shoulder tattoos that were indecipherable.

The mother and the girl lived on Seminole in a house that was all shutters. A house that always looked like nobody was home even if somebody was. Seminole, even by just its name, was not a road I played on or even walked or rode my bike down, except fast, to get somewhere, and not looking to either side, only looking at the yellow line.

My mother had a name for what was wrong with the girl, but my name for it, for what the girl was, or for what she had come to be, or always had been, was "Seminole."

The mother had invited me to come over for cookies,

lemon bars and whatnot. I figured I could chew whatever they offered without swallowing. I figured I could stay standing in the doorway, say my *Thank yous* quickly, take whatever they wanted to give me and go.

The mother took the girl with her everywhere.

I went to the fair alone.

I bought a corndog, an elephant ear, a bunny—and, well, I really only wanted to take the one bunny, but the farmer had talked me into taking the mother rabbit too so as not to separate kin.

I kept picturing the mother of the girl with a plastic container of cookies, holding it out to me. Their house on the inside lit by lamps with yellowed shades, a blue corduroy couch, framed butterflies, dust. The girl—drooling.

I just never showed.

I just heard this: the mother of the girl saying to the mothers, to whomever she came across, to my mother—that I had thrown, that she had seen me throwing, either rocks or stones at her girl.

Let me just say to you now so that there is no confusion, that I never learned to swim, that I cannot swim.

You would have to trust water to swim.

You would have to trust anything.

The vet had said, holding the frayed ear of the dead bunny, "Yes, yes, really strangulation, but these marks are not dog. These marks were made by another rabbit."

In the car on the ride home, my mother and I decided it would be best to blame the dog, anyway.

To everybody we told, we blamed the dog.

To the breastless lady I blamed the dog. She said, "Yes, oh, I read, it happens," then she said it wasn't suffocation but that the body temperature of bunnies is controlled through their ears. "The poor thing must have just burned up," she said, her tattooed husband nodding.

It would have been then, when they were out there floating. It would have been then that I might have gotten up a handful of rocks and pebbles and even some of that water-softened glass and thrown it underhand, arching it, so that the handful rained down onto the girl like hail.

During dinner and throughout the unair-conditioned evenings my mother and I were mostly asking each other if the rabbit could have known what gnawing on her bunny's ears like that would do—had done.

After the bunny died the rabbit starved herself to death—after all that chewing she stopped eating altogether.

This death too we blamed on the dog.

When my mother heard about the stones she said, "It's *helluhtious!*" She said, "Go get me my cigarettes."

My mother did not take me with her all the time.

My mother had a diamond necklace she never took off.

She had cigarettes. She played mah-jongg.

She made me lunch. Peanut butter and banana sandwiches or thin-sliced ham, every day.

In the lake on the raft, when they were boating sometimes, their black hair stuck to their faces.

In summer on Fridays my mother came home with freshly painted fuchsia fingernails, and when I looked at them, holding her hands in my hands, to look at them, she said, "Blood Melon."

Every day at dusk the girl swam out to the buoy.

Then every day the mother and the girl made their way home from the beach on that junky old bike with the brakes always rubbing.

Then every day I took myself, my sandy feet, rocks, collected stones, frayed towel, softened pieces of green-glass, a cheerio—home, counting, counting things, anything, rocks, usually backwards.

Then I got home. Then I might get home.

Then I might have fed the bunny and the rabbit.

On the beach in the just starting rain everyone was running for the road home. I was walking. There was no thunder.

I saw down the road the mother and the girl. The mother

trying to hoist the girl into the child's seat on the bike, steadying it. The girl, getting on, getting into her special seat, the mother waiting for her to be in, and what I saw was the rain—the tiniest, diamondy drops, raining, not down on the mother and the girl, but raining up from them.**Q**

The Kind of Story You Write
When You're Stuck in Las Vegas

I call up Corey. I tell Corey how red as a beet I am. I tell Corey my urethra. I tell Corey up all night when Corey asks me do I sleep nights. Then Corey calls me back. Corey tells me that she just asked the doctor for me. Corey says, "This may sound inappropriate to you." Corey means the kind of salve the doctor said that I should get. Corey says, "For a cow." I say, "For a cow?" Corey says, "For their udders when they crack and things." I tell Corey red as a beet. I shout at Corey my urethra, not my udder. I say, "Corey, go ask the doctor why he's crazy." Corey calls me back. Corey says she just asked the doctor for me. Corey says the doctor told her there are plenty of studies on it. Corey says for me not to think about it that it has a picture of a cow on the wrapper. "I am as red as a beet," I shriek. I say, "Corey, look—go ask the doctor right now maybe is there something else I could get for this instead." Corey calls me back. Corey says, "He says no."

No, there is not anything.

I say, "Corey, listen—do you want to look at my urethra?"

Corey says, "Okay, okay, I'll call the grocer."

Some fucking friend.

The whole world, some fucking world. **Q**

Production

From that we go to Waterfalls. All girls appear at the top of Waterfalls. All girls wear one-piece silver suits and silver bathing-caps with a silver chin-strap. All girls slide down Waterfalls, equipped with slicky-slides, straight down into the pool. All girls swim in and out of formations—Snowflake, Ball, Big Sun, Circle. Top-point of fountain emerges from center of Circle. At cue, all girls swim inward until reaching fountain with non-stick foot spaces on every tier. Fountain continues to emerge, a fountain of silver-capped girls in silver one-pieces reaching higher into sky then Waterfalls, which has faded to black. At cue, girls dive from fountain, tier by tier, into pool. All girls swim outward until returning to Circle, turning it clockwise until fountain is once again submerged. Back to Big Sun, Ball, and all girls finish up with Snowflake, while behind them Waterfalls, which is built on turnstiles, changes to Arctic. Snowflake goes to Circle, which breaks in one place as soon as one girl lets go. All girls swim in a chain around to the back of Arctic to be met on stairs by costumers with skis, poles, parkas, and down-to-the-waist, silver-white wigs. Pool closes up. All girls undo chin-straps. All girls appear at the top of Arctic. All girls ski down Arctic on snow until reaching snowy bottom where all girls perform finale. Finale is choreographed for ski, pole, and wig. Big Sun, Ball, Snowflake, Ball, Big Sun, Snowflake, Circle. All girls drop skis, poles, wigs, parkas into center of Circle. One long chain. Girls, all dark (ropes come down), a silver star on every nipple (lifted up with ropes). Darkness and stars lifting. All girls holding on. **Q**

JASON SCHWARTZ

A Grammar

I would touch a spot on the sheet.

I would touch the windows and the grass, the rip beneath the trees, by the boat—which, indeed, was sinking. The mountain in the bracken was the face, and pleasant, pertaining also to the pitter-patter in the walls, to farce, that is to say, at least inasmuch as the headboard was oxblood, but not old, and the door, of a sudden, was open.

The water pitcher, given an accident of the shadows, resembled a woman—the fact of which recalls, oddly, the little book in the bookcase, a grammar, or, at any rate, the coats in the closet—and the woman who, quietly, parenthetically, oh, yes, later on, at the end, said your name.

I would touch the spot that felt like skin, the shards of thread on the part that made his arms, the horsehair stuck through the mountain and the fields—which were quite black in aspect, it now seems. I would touch where it was warm, it is true, the crease loose, my sleeve a little clumsy, a little bunched and to the side—worn, in short, poorly, the tumbler like so, the moment undone.

The birch trees are indistinct. (It is dusk, after all.) There is a lawn. (Wrought-iron gate, lamps.) A fellow calls to a dog. (The mailbox stands next to the fence.) An automobile passes. (You will note, just the same, the walk, the dark pots, the benches.) Mrs. Schwartz tends to the flowers. (Now she turns, and we cannot see her anymore.)

One considers the pattern, frets over it.

The interval, you will agree, is droll.

The soldier, whose boots are shining, the wool of whose uniform is blue, rides beyond the farmhouse—which is ablaze.

The man, the woman, are off to town, possibly—to buy, one likes to think, eggs and such, buttermilk, sugar, a loaf of bread.

There is something bedeviling about the error. The bonnet, for instance, is apparent and then hidden. Oh, there is a sort of trill, one confesses—and, why, a dwindling.

A curtain rustles somewhat. (It is the cat, of course.) Music plays. (*Falstaff*, or something to this effect.) Doors are opened and closed. (Earrings sit upon an end-table.) Objects are clutched, arranged, observed. (The moon—to digress—is gone.)

The chifforobe, upon which was emblazoned, in red, a lake scene (birds—apple trees), and upon a shelf of which would sit his cuff links, stood next to the night table—and at some remove from the window. The bed was a curious example of the Colonial four-poster style, one is told, on account of the claw-and-ball feet—and the squeal, in a manner of speaking, in the frame.

The quilt was kept at the foot, at the posts, or, to be precise, where I had made the rows of trees and pickets his legs on the sheet. The chair, which was maple-wood, and scuffed rather variously, had embroidered arms and a discolored rib, and sat next to the bed, yes, against the wall—through which, you understand, would sometimes come a bit of this or that.

There are ducks and boats. (Gifts, after all.) The bookcase is black. (The windowsill is brown.) The chifforobe stands across from the closet. (There are collars, buttons, shoes.) Pictures hang above the desk. (Elephants and knots, plainly.) The door is open. (You will note, moreover, the flannel, the hole.)

He pulls the sheet to my neck. **Q**

Why Hemingway Killed Himself

The dog (my dog) weighs 65 pounds. The cat (our cat) weighs 7 or 8 pounds. The refrigerator weighs 125 pounds or so. There's a washing machine, it weighs 90 pounds. Maybe more. The dryer weighs 75 pounds, also maybe more. My lawyer weighs 190 pounds. The toaster weighs 1 pound. The lawn mower weighs 43 pounds. My wife weighs 130 pounds. Our bed weighs 100 pounds, mattress and box spring included. Our bed with my wife in it weighs 230 pounds. These are estimates, you understand. This pencil I'm using, it weighs next to nothing, I guess. The televisions weigh 40 pounds a piece; that's 120 pounds. My daughter weighs 45 pounds. My wife's doctor weighs 175 pounds. My father weighs 240 pounds. One of my brothers weighs 2,000 pounds. I myself have no weight at all, and am blown across lawns and yards by the slightest stir of breeze. **Q**

Choke Chain

They slept like dogs above the kitchen. In hanging boxes he had made for them from old yellow planks, boxes open-topped and high-sided—this is where the boys slept, legs twitching. There was never any barking in this house. There was only the creak of the boys over our heads as they slept and the sounds of the sister, the oldest one, the point–faced sister still called by her baby name, pawing through the night by herself.

There was a narrow boardwalk he had made after finishing the quiet, creaking boxes for the boys. The boardwalk slats had been laid as tracks from room to room and we heard the padding of the sister on the wood of them while the sleeping boys were breathing and turning in their boxes and this place was hot with darkness and steaming with the people in it.

These nights he would cover me with stones. Round, heavy granites and soft–coated slates, cool on my skin, warm from so much dark, and sometimes bricks brought in just before night and piled in piles he would show me and say: you.

The boys were easy, boxed against each other as they were and happy enough with the walks and the food and all the dark woods for chase or hunt or catch, but it was the hard sister, the first one to come, she was always the one sniffing down the boardwalk in the night, scratching to get at the bits of things that had fallen below.

It was after the play–tired boys were put down, settled each into his own box, curved in with scraps of linen and old shirts and thin pillows breathing feathers, that we would hear the sister closer, her breath coming in loose–jawed puffs, making the noises she would make in the kitchen beneath the sleeping boys. We heard the slide of her against painted walls, and through the door he closed behind me we felt the shaking quiet of her listening.

These nights, because in this place there were always more

nights, I stayed where he put me, on wood or on carpet, stand-ing, squatting, kneeling, him in the chair and the sound of the sis-ter always sharply boardwalk—crouching to catch the breath of dark air from this room that slipped out through the finger space under the door.

Sometimes it was the smell of the branches, fresh yew and fir, the smell of the dark and living things cut by him into me with the curve—bladed knife, the cut and bloodied smell of the out-side inside me, enough smell to wake the boys to whimper in their boxes and set the sister to pacing and scraping at the door.

From the place I was now I remembered the place I used to sleep, in the room past the last of the narrow–slatted boardwalk, the room of skin and cotton and soft–rounded pillows heavy with feathers. I remembered the look of it, squared, small–bedded and pale, filled with the drawers he had made, drawers round–knobbed and deep, set one above the other, set into walls and set into closets, smooth–sliding, scented paper drawers, filled and shut and silent and everything in them mine. I was the color of tea then. I was warm and sheer and pooling into the low places left by the weighted limbs of bodies in my small bed.

This night there was field wire. Crossed and knotted four–point stars, darker than this night was dark, curved and uncurving from the coil at his feet, until I was only sound. The knifing, breathy sound of wire through air, the fast-ripped sound of some-thing that had once been mine, and all the throat-made sounds of me in this place, this is what I was.

This was the night the boys ran, hitting hard down the dark with the strong heaving of their sides, howling and clawing and pushing out into the woods. I heard the sound of their leaving from my place in this room, heard the thinning of their cries through the sheer stretch of night between us.

This was the night the sister scratched long down the door of this place. This was the night we heard her begging me. **Q**

Mother

I go to the window and look out down the street. I am standing one story up looking out down the road. I aim the telescope a few blocks up to the retirement tower and then up ten floors. I stop at her window. Her curtains are drawn.

Twenty-eight floors of drawn curtains.

I leave the telescope aimed at the window and step back. The phone rings. I pick up the wrist rocket on the table next to the telescope. I pull back the little leather pocket. I don't answer the phone because she has just come out of her apartment building and is heading down the street toward the tower. She is late. The machine answers the call. I hear myself saying I am not able to take the call right now, please leave a message.

"I know you're watching me," she says into the machine. "Sick little man," she says and then she coughs and hangs up—laughing, coughing, mostly coughing, then hanging up.

I call her back.

"Now what?" is how she answers.

"Okay," I tell her, "just a few minutes."

"Thank you, sweetheart," she says, and asks if maybe I would like to see her naked. I laugh into the phone and stretch the rubber cord of the wrist rocket. "Kiss, kiss," she says.

I hang up.

I step out onto the porch. It's one of those Sunday mornings—peaceful, sunny, warm.

Serene and misleading.

As I look over the neighborhood, something shakes and hacks and wakes between two houses across the street. The wind blows and the stale smell of the taverns drifts past me and around the flat. Cars line both sides of the road. Most of them are labeled with orange parking tickets. Some have been tagged for towing. They are all heaps. One of those tagged for towing has no driver's-side window and is double-parked. The passenger side door is open and a pair of legs hangs out onto the road. I go back in the house and aim the telescope down the street. Three blocks up I find her. She adjusts a brassiere strap and her purse slides off her shoulder. She pulls the purse up, annoyed, adjusts her cardigan sweater around her hips. The dog a few houses down begins to bark and does not stop. It's tied up, wrapping and unwrapping its chain around the post, barking. I get the wrist rocket and steelies. The first shot only makes a puff in the dirt next to the dog. The dog looks over at the dust, shakes its head, jangles the chain. The dog takes a step toward the dissolving puff of dirt, its neck stretched.

The second shot makes more than dust.

The dog shuts up, its tail drops between its legs and it looks around, scared, suspicious, sniffing.

Things start to happen. Curtains and sheets begin to get pulled back from the windows of some of the houses. Men with bellies step outside, shirtless. A child in a diaper toddles down the sidewalk alone. I notice she has disappeared, gone into the retirement complex, is riding the elevator, is walking into her room, adjusting her brassiere strap, pushing her hair back.

"Tell me what you know," she says.

"Know?" I say.

"I've got your number," she says. "I'll get your name."

I step over to the telescope and look up at the window in the retirement complex. The curtain is open. She is standing there looking out. She is looking the wrong way. "I'm not there, sweetheart," I say to her, though only in my mind and not out loud.

"Who is this?" I ask.

She removes an earring, annoyed. "Why have you been calling?" she says.

"Who's calling who?" I say.

"You know what I'm talking about," she says, slipping out of her cardigan in front of the window. She hangs up and stands there in the window, the phone in one hand, her cardigan in the other. She stands there in her tank top. She opens the window. I step away from the telescope and make sure the machine is on, ready to take messages. The dog starts barking. This time it barks at the child in the diaper, the toddler toddling, unsupervised, aware, unaware. A woman comes out of a house in her bathrobe. The bathrobe is turquoise and orange. She holds her bathrobe closed as she goes after the child. The tow truck arrives. The two men who came in the tow truck are unaware of the legs hanging out onto the road. They raise the car and are ready to pull away. Then one of them gets out and pulls on the feet until the rest of the person is lying on the street. The man gets back in the truck. The truck goes away. The dog turns and barks, snaps at the air. The woman in the turquoise and orange bathrobe grabs the toddler by the hand and swings it around in the air. She is still standing at the window in her tank top. She is smoking.

"Smoking's bad for you," I say.

I hang up.

The phone rings. I get the wrist rocket. The dog barks. I go out onto the porch and take aim. There is a puff of dust near the dog and the dog looks around. She is standing at the window, putting on her sweater. She closes the window and slips her purse over her shoulder.

"Now what?" she says.

"Suit yourself," she says, and is gone, turned into a dial tone.

I go outside, walk down the street. I get cigarettes and steelies at the Quick Mart up on the corner. Jesus stops me outside the store. "Hey Jack," he says, "a buck for Jesus?" I tell Jesus to get out of my goddamn way before I nail him to a telephone pole. Only I don't say this out loud.

My machine has a message.

I look through the telescope and see the old lady staring out the window. She must be sitting down now because that's all that's in the window, is her head.

I unplug the phone. I unplug the machine. I go out on the porch with the wrist rocket. I take aim. There is the snap of the wrist rocket and the whiz of the steelie and then there is a crack and the dog collapses and lies there, unmoving, not barking.

Twenty-two misses and four hits. **Q**

CHRISTINE SCHUTT

The Enchantment

Someone else was in the room, I think—the second wife. High-parted hair, lips absently applied—the second wife had been the one to go on talking to my grandfather. Not the first, the first left licking salt from the wide rim of her glass; the third, we knew, was spending Daddy's money. My grandfather said to me, "We wanted you to hear this," and I think, I remember it happening this way, there was another in the room, not just my father and my grandfather but my father's second wife.

We were told—my grandfather told us, speaking to me, "Your father is tired; he needs a rest."

I saw the head of my father's head fall forward—monk's bald spot, mad curls. Broad, broad-hearted, rufous chest, a squalling red—my father was alive and in the world and feeling everything extremely, feeling everything that could be felt.

Did she move to touch him, the blur behind, whoever else was in the room—because I didn't. In the face of that face then lifted to me, I smiled to hear him name a place, which when I heard it . . . I might even have been there or else my memory is so profligate and willfully confused, but I think I always knew this place where my father was going. In a long car that gentled over the grated threshold, my grandfather took him, and, some time, me, past swells of lawn and more lawn, wind and slashes of high blue sky in the heads of furious trees. Odd men they were I saw standing in the spiny leaves pinching winter berries; bent-over figures in discourse with the air. How could my father sleep here—I wanted to know, but the second wife was in the car, too, saying it was hard to be surprised this way, come upon by family.

"Visitors is what we are. We won't stay long," my grandfather said, and we made it through the lunch when we saw the other slinkers in the damp, strawed beds, heard them call, "Professor!"

bow and smirk; and I thought—he seemed to me pleased, my father, until he turned to ask, "Why this?"

"Why what?" my grandfather asked. "Tell me what. What are you asking? What is it you want? Do you know what you want? Do you know what you are doing?"

My grandfather said, "You have no idea," but my father kept behind, speaking rapidly, voice soft, my father asking why when the windows whirred up, and he was left turning in the turn-around to see us go. A man in a short robe, left unsashed, how did it feel to him, I wondered, the worried, furrowed inside seam of his short robe's pocket?

In the coats he left behind, I had gritted my nails on the inside seams of father's pockets, gritted and sucked them clean.

I did not see him then for a time that passed in the way of winter, colorless and stubbled and flat. The days clicked past same as hangered linens from my grandfather's laundress, underwear cupped in puffs next to slips—my own, only my own, nothing of my father's the way it had been when we shared in the last house a dresser, a closet, a bathroom down the hall.

My father knocking, I sometimes heard and remembered. "What?" Grandfather said, "You must remember what?"

"See here," my grandfather said to the company—not her, but men like my grandfather with vacation faces, smooth and oiled and brown. Same suits, thin cuffs, glint of heavy watches when they signed. Here and here and here—so many papers.

"What am I a party to?" she asked when she arrived, knife-pleated skirt and filmy blouse, spectacles for reading, a pair for seeing out.

"This," my grandfather said, as surely as he cleared his throat or pulled at his eccentric too-big clothing; and the second wife came to where we stood hooding our eyes from the dazzle at the window. Water from such a height was a dizzying coin—that, and the hard shore, the palings of trees, and closer to the house, at our feet from the window, the raw paving of my grandfather's terrace—his, the benches, the paths to the garden—a stony estate designed to withstand winters that cracked the very roads, to whom now would all of this be given.

I didn't quite ask, really; just, "How much do you have, Grandfather? For how long has this been yours?"

My grandfather said for as long as he remembered. He was born in the bedroom where he once slept with a wife. He said, "I have always been comfortable."

I wanted to be comfortable.

In the sun room with the easy men in pearly colors, I spoke freely of my father and of what I had seen with and without wives, waking to my father in his sleepless disarray, a man in tears, kissing my foot and saying I had saved him—my father always threatening death—rolled playbill in his pocket, at my face his sugared breath: we should, we should.

"Yes," she said. "I have seen him with her in this way and been afraid." His temper, for one, as when the milk had boiled over—scalded; and of course, he wouldn't drink it, but argued through the rising light before he took his sleep. "Insomniacs," she said, "are true accountants; they are smug about the time they keep. But he sold the family silver," she said.

"He is not rich," my grandfather said.

I did not tell them what my father had bought me, but I wore the earrings and the small, slight clothes he had said I would grow into—and I had. Even as my grandfather spoke, I was lifting off elastic from where it pinched me.

Breasts, my own.

Breasts, hands, long thin feet and water-thinned soles—mine, walking the cold stones of my grandfather's terrace, the cold knocking me just behind the knees—every time; but not so with her, the second wife in broken shoes, a generous sweater; she was warm.

She asked, "Did you wonder if I knew?"

I had wondered was there other breathing in the room, a greater dark near the doorway rimmed in downstairs light, and which wife standing, the second, third, or first—in this way alike, watching or sometimes driving for him when Daddy said he could not concentrate to drive—made sick by just the entrance at Grandfather's gate.

"Was it for money that we came here?" I asked—all those Sunday dinners with the slavering roast sliced bloody on the tines of the carving tools, Grandfather's rare meat and garden vegetables, not the lunch we had on visits to my father's last new place, but Sunday dinner and the long, white afternoon in a room where we sat reading until supper.

Quiet, the gaping stairways still and cold, cold air hissing through the sills, the rooms I looked into were dark and cold except for where my grandfather was reading Sunday's papers after the visit to my father; or it might have been after the visit from the pearly men—or any Sunday really it might have been that we were alone, long years alone, my grandfather and I, the wives fled and the cook's night off, so that what were we to do but what we did? We took the afternoon's roast, and it seems to me this happened, my grandfather gave me a knife and fork and said, "Take what you want," and we cut into the bleedy meat and picked at it standing, not bothering with plates with no one there to scold for what we did, pouring salt into a spoon of juice and drinking meat, red enough it still said, "Ouch!" at a prick from the tines of my Grandfather's enormous bone-handled fork.

My nails were grimed with cinder, my lips a smear of grease.

Complicitous season, winter, the day blacked on a sudden as did the hallway from my room to his, and we often did not make a visit to my father. We often stayed at home, saying we would only have to turn around again, and so we did not visit—or phone as my father complained to me, brushing his lips against the mouthpiece of the phone, voice over-ocean on the holidays' connections, sometimes cut off.

The way my father talked! Tremulous show-off, he was, all fustian to-do when in the last new place we saw him with his friends, the same we always caught peeking in on us together. "Still here!" my father said as if another place were possible.

"Come in, please, come in." We were introduced again, but I re-member no one's name. Even the faces are gone. We had come to see my father. Grandfather and I—and sometimes the second wife—we hadn't driven this far just to shake some soft hands.

"So why bother?" we agreed, and I often didn't see my father. Easy to make excuses in the gaudy life—fourteen, fifteen, six-teen—riding on my way somewhere and smoking a cigar, stink-ing up the driver's daddy's car.

"I live here," I said by way of a good night at my grandfather's door, yet forgetful of the driveway lights, which shone through falling snow, pooling white on white when next I saw them.

Morning, my grandfather at the table talked of lights left on. He said, "You are not with your father. There are rules in this house, remember," rules I was told my father never followed—which was why then. The inexorable logic, how hard I worked to live by it as Grandfather's darling. No thank you, no I couldn't, no please to what he took from Daddy to give to me.

Petting my watch on any Sunday's visit, my father said to me, "So the old man won't die with it still on his wrist." Lucid on the subject of anyone's belongings, noticing the second wife's new rings, my father seemed alert to the getting. The shadow boxes and the canes, the grandfather clock, the shoe horns, the brushes, the studs, the links, the pins—such enameled old blue—my father knew the history to and wanted them. He said so. My father said to my grandfather, "When were you last dancing?"

My grandfather's smile had teeth for this part. Such things as he had were his to give, which he did when he was not afraid of dying—or so my father said. My father said to my grandfa-ther, "Maybe not dancing, but traveling, are you thinking of traveling again?" To the places I had seen in photographs—Grandfather backdropped by the walleyed rams at Karnak—would he travel there again, as once he had, a young man in a high collar, unused to such heats yet smiling?

Upright before whatever scene the camera found him, my grandfather had traveled, had been to, had seen the famous cities before the modern wars rubbled them. He had plundered the shops famous for their porcelains and brought home plate and platter and sconce. The teardropped chandelier above the table where we ate, and the canes, of course, from London. I heard him speak. Those are Portuguese, those Italian, but the bronze Diana—oh, God, who knows from where? "I bought it," he said, "but your grandmother was embarrassed by the figure's upturned breasts. Your grandmother," he said, "you can imagine how she suffered your father's first attack, the second—all those wives."

Grandfather's disappointment, I could hear it in his voice when he said his good-nights, the way the words came out words—and was it with some longing—and for what from a man who had had and had? Mistresses, my father told me, he had glimpsed in the crowds of the company parties, ladling the punch, stacking plates high with sandwiches. "My poor mother," my father said.

Sometimes on our Sunday visits my father cried to remember her. "Mother, Mother," he said while my grandfather looked on and the second wife coughed, embarrassed.

The way my father dressed, grown fat from too much sleeping, in mismatched clothes, seedy as a poet, now he knew himself as poor—and happy to be poor. Look how he was loved, and he pointed to the men who swayed at his door with, "Professor James, sir, may we come in, please?"

"Don't ask them in," I said. "Be someone different."

Be one of the the boys at the concerts, at the ceremonies, at the breakfasts. They rarely spoke of my father, or if they did, it was, "How's Jim?" How was it at this last new place? Expensive as hell was what my grandfather said, but we wanted him well again—didn't we?

My grandfather said, "Poor Jim."

The second wife said, "Of all the men." She said, "I gave him you, didn't I?"

But everything we did, I thought, we did for money.

In my grandfather's house, I was given the room with the western view that lit up the matchstick winter trees, a book's worth at a strike—wasteful, too early, short. Winter afternoons, pitched in dark, we sometimes slept in the library, lap-robed in Sunday's papers, my grandfather snoring clogged snores from stories. Warty giants who lived in caves beyond the umbered forest, my grandfather was like one of those in his sleep or that was how I saw him if I was first to wake. I saw the large, sore nose, its old-age red and the rest of him brown-speckled like an egg, and yet I kissed him.

"Too much," my grandfather said. "That's enough."

There was more he was saying except I moved away with my part of the paper, which was never Grandfather's part of the paper. His part of the paper was nothing to read.

My father said he could not read. He said, "Now they've got me on this stuff, I can't concentrate. I can't see. All I do is sleep."

I had never seen my father asleep, never known him to be other than fever-pitch awake; flame-tip skin and heat I had felt from his fingers at my cheeks. Not afraid of touching, my father was not, and his roiled speech—sometimes hard to follow what he said. "These drugs," he said. "It's not my fault"—anymore than he was here in this last new place. "My own father," my father said. "He did this to me."

"Did what?" I asked. Left alone sometimes in his room to talk, we talked about my grandfather: hard as the stony place that he had made into a home—and me in it. What was he doing with me on the estate was the question.

My father lifted at the skirt of his short robe. He asked, "What does he want from you?"

I scratched him.

"You would think we were lovers," he said, and I hit at his arms, pushed at his chest with the heels of my hands, pushed at the softening parts—at his belly. He laughed and then grew angry and slapped small slaps fast, all over me until I was backed up against the door and crying—surely, a snotty, messy kind of crying, the body in an ooze, although what I remember is the joy I felt to call my father fucker, you fucker.

I told my grandfather, "I wish I were yours." Almost any Sunday I said it. Even if the second wife were present as she sometimes was, I said, "I never want to live with my father again." The second wife thought it best, too. In my grandfather's house there was routine: Cook's soft-boiled egg in the morning and a table-set dinner each night. Not as it had been with Daddy, the second wife was sure of this, how it was with my father—she had known me eating at the sink from a bag, school shoes still missing and late for school—yet she had let my father drive me.

"Good-bye. See you later. See you next Sunday, next month, next year. You wouldn't want me to give up work. None of this, of course, means I don't love you. Remember how it was. You understand. This is better." Any one of us could have said as much.

Besides, I wanted every morning to break up buttered toast into the Royal Doulton eggcup.

I wanted lots and lots of new clothes.

Keys to the car, plane ticket, passport, backstage passes.

I wanted to be between visits on a Saturday alone when we walked Grandfather's gardens—him with the pruners in his pocket and a cane he used to beat at things while he pruned in rolled-up sleeves. The steeped-tea color of my grandfather's arms, sure in every gesture, aroused me. I wanted to brush against and lick him: the pouch at his neck, his white, white hair. Stooped, skinny, abrupt in motion, loose clothes slipping off, my grandfather used his pruners. He worked beneath a weak sun and did not sweat or smell of anything more than his ordered soap, green bars with age cracks that looked like saved stones from the bottom of the lake. The lake, from whichever angle we looked, was chipped blues or grays, or buckled, as with ice; and when it was ice, we stayed indoors. We watched for winter birds—blood smears in the trees or the blue jays he detested swinging on the onion sacks and pecking at the suet. The snow was dirty; shucks of seed skirted the trees. There were pawprints and footprints and dog's canary piddle—too many visitors on any one day.

I'm sorry, I get confused.

The snows that filled the wells of ground about my

grandfather's gardens were unmarked and falling in the lights I thoughtlessly left on.

My father was sick and had been sick for as far back as my grandfather could remember.

Imagine what it was like to have a son who said such things!

But what my father said about me! I had heard him before on how it was with me—me, a hole, a gap, a breach, a space, an absence and longing. Empty. Feckless. Stupid.

"Who can ever fill you up?" my father asked.

Then I was using something sharp on him, just to draw a little blood. I was being showy and so was he, my father—he knew about acting. He was smiling while I cut him, so that it must have been the second wife who screamed—not me. Why would I have screamed? My grandfather in the room saw what I was doing. **Q**

Dialogue

"Do you want to know what I think?" he said.

"No," she said. "I do not."

"What I mean," he said, "is you do need to know what I think, don't you?"

"No," she said, "not really."

"I don't think you understand," he said.

"Yes," she said, "I do understand."

"You don't really get it, do you?"

"There is nothing to get," she said.

"What do you mean," he said, "'nothing to get'?"

"You know what I mean," she said.

"No, I do not," he said. "Tell me."

"There is nothing to tell," she said.

"I do not understand," he said. "I need you to tell me."

"You do not need me to tell you," she said.

"Yes, I do," he said. "I want to know."

"You do not want to know," she said.

"But I do, I do," he said. "I do want to know. Please," he said, "please tell me. I need you to tell me what you think." **Q**

Help Me!

I heard someone scream last night At first, I thought it was a kid. Then I realized it was a woman. It was faint, but unmistakable. I looked out my window, which happened to be open, because I'd just cooked a hamburger. I couldn't see anything because it was fogged up. I was wiping it with my hand when I heard her scream, "Help me!" She only said this once. *Help me.* Maybe she was out on the street. Maybe someone was robbing her. I would have run downstairs immediately, but I was wearing socks.

I thought about putting my shoes on.

But by that time everything was quiet.

"Did you hear someone screaming?" I called out my window to a man who was shoveling snow off a car. The man just shook his head. Maybe he was too winded to speak. I turned off all my lights so I could see better into the other apartments. Somebody's legs were up on a coffee table. One floor up, a woman thoughtfully paced her apartment with a bottle of beer in her hand. Every time she took a sip, she looked at herself in the mirror. I thought about calling the police, but then I thought it was probably a couple having a bad fight, and then they had patched things up.

The next day I bought a newspaper. I wanted to be sure there wasn't any blood on my hands, as they say. But there was a rape, and it had happened around the time I heard the scream. The story was on page three. A woman had been dragged into a car. She had been to the movies by herself and she was walking home. She was walking on the sidewalk by the Saul Solomon Field—a park with a couple of baseball diamonds. The man got out of his car and chased her. She screamed, but no one came. Instead of running into the road, she ran into the park, where there was no light, and no one to help her. He ran after her and caught her and put his hand over her mouth and dragged her into the car. He was driving a Ford Escort. But I was certain that this was not the woman I had heard. The park was much too far away from my apartment for me to have heard anything. A good ten-minute walk, if you were walking really fast.

I had to go to the park to see where it had happened. The paper didn't give the exact location, but it was easy to tell. There were a bunch of footprints in the snow, and these were the only footprints in the entire park. No one else had set foot in there since the snowstorm.

"There's no way you could have heard her," my best friend Mike said when I called him and told him about it. "It's like ten football fields away from you—and, besides, there's a lot of snow—it cuts down noise."

"But it's not out of the question?" I said.

"No," he said. "I mean yes. It is out of the question. A bomb could explode down there and you wouldn't hear it."

"What about the wind?" I said. "It was windy last night. Maybe you can hear someone whisper a mile away if the wind does something freaky."

"Why do you care, anyway?" he said.

"If that was her voice," I said, "it'll stay with me forever."

I asked Mike to do me a favor. I asked him to walk down there and at precisely five minutes past the hour for him to go ahead and scream, "Help me!"

"Are you crazy?" he said. "People are going to stare at me."

I begged him. I told him I'd buy him a couple of beers. He said he'd do it for a six-pack of Ipswich Ale. We synchronized our watches and hung up.

I stood by my window and waited. I had some time. He wouldn't be there for another ten minutes. "You really get worked up over everything," I said to myself. Five minutes passed. I kept looking at my watch. My palms were getting sweaty. Then there was one minute to go. In fifty seconds he was going to scream it. I told myself I wouldn't be able to hear a thing, that when Mike got home he'd call me and probably say something sarcastic like, "Are you satisfied?" I pictured Mike standing there, looking annoyed, ready to scream, "Help me!" Or maybe, knowing him, he wouldn't scream this at all—he'd just tell me he had. Perhaps he wasn't even there. He could have been at home looking at his watch. But it didn't matter, did it? I put my fingers in my ears. I started talking nonstop. I started naming everything in the room. I used a loud voice.

I said, "This is my chair. This is my carpet. This is my wall, my walls, all my walls."

I was worried I was going to run out of things to name.

It sounded to me as if I was shouting underwater.

"That's my stereo. Those are my books. This is my room. I'm sorry. I'm sorry. I'm sorry. I'm sorry." **Q**

CAROL DE GRAMONT

The Lost Breast

All she could do was raise one arm, and she raised it now, asking it to give her a boost out of bed. But the arm made a brief, fluttering arc, and then flapped, exhausted, onto the sheet. So she went on lying there, on her back, in the dark, watching the light seeping in from somewhere, from under the door perhaps, the pinkish light showing her the shape of the bed. She could see how pale the bed was, could feel how cool it was, but she could not see much else, could not, for instance, see the door. There was a shadowy thing—a curtain or a screen, something like that—looming at her feet, blocking her view of the door.

How she wanted to see the door, to know if it was open or closed. She thought she would like to know who was making the sounds outside, there in the hallway—tinny sounds, shushing voices, a strange clattering of wheels. If she could just call out to the persons in the hallway, to please come into the room and help her get to her feet and make her way from the bed. Or to come to tell her, please, why she could not do this for herself.

It was then that she heard the scream. It sounded to her as if an animal were screaming, as if something alive were being tortured out in the backyard or in the woods behind it. She tried to get her head raised off the pillow. Perhaps she could see the window; weren't the screams coming from outside it? But it was hopeless; she could not get her head up, could see nothing over there, where the window was, except a wall of peltish gloom.

She heard a rustling and crashing as if through leaves— through the pachysandra bed, she supposed it was—and again, the scream. And again she heard it. The scream was always the same: a long and spiraling shriek followed by a faint, almost pleading groan. Or a croak or a gasp. It was the sound, say, of an animal responding to claws tearing deep, mortally deep, into its chest.

A cat, of course, was doing the torturing, she thought; what other kind of animal would be outside tormenting its prey in the dead of night? But the animal getting itself tortured: what kind of creature was it? How odd it was, she thought, that somewhere outside some creature, probably a bird, something, some poor thing was being tortured by another thing and she could not determine what the thing being tortured was.

Or where it was. For now the screams seemed to be bursting not from the backyard but from above the ceiling: from the roof, the gutters, or the eaves. She lay still, listening to the dreadful racket, picturing night-hawks raiding a wrens' nest in the eaves, the hawks' yard-wide wings and snatching talons swooping ominously across the roof. But this was absurd, she reflected, recalling that birds of prey did their killing quickly, and in silence, except for the slight rustling of wings.

Yet so vivid were the swooping hawks in her mind that when she felt the air stirring above her bed—no more than a cool breath, really—she thought of feathery wings circling just below the ceiling. And then the next hideous scream, the next plaintive groan, sounded uncannily close to the bed. Could the window be open? she wanted to know. Could the wretched things, whatever they were, have gotten themselves inside the room? Again she tried to get her head raised off the pillow, and this time she did it, got her head raised up just enough to look at the window.

What she saw out there was not the boxy blackness of the bedroom windows, nor the unlit backyard and the woods behind it, but the savage red glow of the city sky at night. She saw the murderous emanations of heat and brick, of immense buildings, of electric lights oozing a palette that looked to her like lymph and blood.

Now she understood where she was—she was up there, in that place. Too high up to hear screams coming from down there, from the distant city street. There was no backyard, of course, no leaves to rustle or crash through. No beds of pachysandra. No stalking cats, no dying birds. There was only the sleek, paved street of the city down there—black, gleaming, merciless.

She fluttered her hand, the good hand, to her spent throat. Then, croaking one last feeble croak, she fell asleep. **Q**

Monuments

So Donald died you know. Turns out Donald and his cigars were not as mutual as Donald claimed, and here Donald had always predicted something less pedestrian would grab him, something magically modern maybe or perhaps a rabid spaniel.

Some kid peed in the hole—in Donald's grave hole, I mean.

Yes, he did, and I do not know who it was. Donald was such a priss—and you know what I mean when I say priss—that the end must have been—pardon the expression, please—just a killer. At his apartment, for instance, where we gathered beforehand—no, there was no hospice for Donald—you know Donald—I smelled pus. Yes, right there at his great old place, which used to be such a circus, there was for a fact, the stink of pus. I know it was. Listen, I know pus when I smell pus.

No, I don't smoke, and I'm glad because I'd have to very often anyway stand outside.

I am not lying about the kid pissing. It was the damnedest thing. Donald's mother said afterward that she didn't mind so much, wasn't really even surprised, but she wondered who he was and why he did it. I told her I had no answers, and Donald's mother wished she at least knew his name. I said, "Well, look, you know Donald, and you must admit he had a legion of lovers and haters."

Sure, I said "a legion." But look, you, skip all of that stuff, there's more. There was a backhoe. Oh, yes, a backhoe. After the kid had pissed himself dry, someone started a backhoe. So it was even worse than the pissing kid. You really should have been there. Donald would have loved it, of course: some young buster barely old enough to shave his chin pissing on the casket, and then a big wonking machine going at it on another grave right next door—wait, is that correct? Can you say *next door* when it comes to graves?

No, it was not me pissing on Donald! Yes, the bucket was big and wide. My guess is a little wider than a casket, and it had welded to it sharp, metal teeth.

You're right about that, Donald's death was an event. It really was, what with the preacher joking and the kid pissing and the backhoe thundering along. Man, it was really churning dirt, that backhoe was. I watched closely, and I could tell the dirt was packed hard because the fellow operating the backhoe had to really goose the gas—or is it diesel with backhoes?—to cut the bucket into the dry ground, to dig below the surface, I mean.

It hasn't rained you know in forever. In fact, the last time it rained really was when you and me and Donald went golfing and Donald fell into the lake trying to chip to the green on the final hole. Was it? I thought it was the final hole. Well, anyway, it rained—I remember that much—and also how you shot about a zillion for a score.

Donald asked me to call you. He asked me when I went by his place with everyone else, when I smelled the pus. Donald said for me to call you and to wish you well.

Hey, no, look, I'm not inventing the backhoe business or the kid either. It sounds phony, but it is completely true. I was there.

Anyway, Donald said to tell our friend—no, that's not right—he said tell "your" friend—yes, that's it—Donald told me to tell you something special. Donald said to come closer, and I did and I smelled the cancer inside of him, blowing in and out of him, oozing and taking over somewhere in there, and Donald said not to let his mother in on this but that I should tell you that you are the best fuck he ever had and he wants you to make something of yourself. He is counting on you to do better than him. He said, "*Tell that gorgeous fuck he makes me sick!*"

We laughed, too, but Donald got to coughing so much and deep that I just could only hold his hand, and his hand was so damn meatless and papery that I needed to kiss it some then, I guess. I was glad I had closed the door during my allotted time. Donald's mother was tactful enough to give me a moment to re-organize my face. She said on the way out that Donald always spoke of me as a friend, and, you know, I just didn't know what to say except I didn't want Donald to die.

What's that? Oh, the backhoe. So the preacher told us at the cemetery that if we had anything to say to Donald then it was time because Donald's physical being—"The vessel of his soul," the preacher said—would soon be buried and therefore unavailable. He said Donald had made an unusual request. The preacher said Donald thought his request to be extremely clever. Seems Donald told the preacher that he had had the final say during his entire life and now he wanted his friends and family to share and enjoy the pleasure.

The preacher said that although he didn't really know Donald very well, he thought Donald handled his fading moments with dignity and grace. The preacher told us Donald called for his mother with his last cough.

The preacher said he usually said *breath* at this point but Donald made him promise to say *cough* instead. A couple of the pallbearers behind me giggled, and the guy next to me said Donald's name softly and put his elbow against mine.

"So step to the side of the grave," the preacher said, "and bid goodbye to a dear man so much loved."

"Please," said the preacher. "Someone. Say goodbye to Donald," he said. And that's when this kid—this young pup with a ponytail—stepped out from behind some of Donald's other friends and walked to the side of the grave. He looked down into the hole. I wondered what he would say, and what I would say when and if I stood there myself. I heard then the odd sound of what turned out to be the kid urinating on the casket. None of us saw this kid actually doing this—his penis peeing, I mean—but it was clear what was going on.

The preacher, who did see the whole thing because he was standing at the end of the grave, said kind of quiet the words *oh* and *my*.

Nobody moved, and the kid posed there, with his hands on his waist, pissing freely, and I thought, Hey, he's pissing on Donald! *He's really pissing on Donald!* I was about to tell the kid to knock it off, to show Donald some respect, when the kid reached down, zipped up, stepped away and then walked into the field of monuments clapping his hands.

I'll say stunned. Donald's mother looked around at the rest of us, and someone behind me said Donald's name again.

The preacher asked if anyone else had anything to say. "Or, for that matter," the preacher said, "to do." And that's exactly when the fellow in the cab of the backhoe shouted at us, tapped his wristwatch and then started up the backhoe's motor. That backhoe began belching black smoke—I guess it is diesel, after all, in those damn machines—and we each of us watched as the gravedigger used small levers with little knobs to dip the bucket onto the ground. It made kind of a ripping sound, the bucket did, in the dry dirt there.

Apparently, none of us had anything to say or do after this, what with the kid and the backhoe, and so the preacher recited a prayer we couldn't hear. We walked away then in groups and singles. No, I didn't look into the grave. I wanted to though. I wanted to see how the urine looked on Donald's casket. I wanted to see if it clung to the surface there. I didn't want that, however, to be my memory of Donald—tiny dots of piss on a long box in a rectangular hole. So I stuck around, and I watched the fellow on the backhoe work open the new grave-site next to Donald. He did not mix the dirt from the new hole with the dirt he would soon scoop over Donald. I watched for some time, and I desired very much then to climb into the cab and take over. I wanted to work the levers there myself. I wanted to hold them in my hands, to feel their quiver, and to perhaps move them a little. I wanted to take a small chew of dirt then and shift the bucket back and forth with it, sprinkling the dirt over the piss I knew was there on top of Donald. I wanted to do this for Donald. I really wanted to do it. But I didn't do anything. **Q**

The Summer of the Dog

What I can't believe is those damned pictures—me sitting on the woodpile, of all the jackass places, me sitting there with not a line of lipstick, looking for all the world rode hard and put up wet like some tenant-farmer wife—slump-shouldered, thin-lipped, washed in worry. The white board wall of the house behind me is grimy with dirt and my neck looks grubby besides. In one of those pictures, he must have said *Smile* because my eyes look out at him, not down, and my lips are straight across. You can see the dark rings circling up from my cheekbones and my fingers gripping down on the logs. No gold whore shoes and red polish there, no fandango dancing, intoxicating, fun-loving thing anywhere in that shot.

There are a mess of those pictures, besides the woodpile ones. There's one of me ironing, of all the fool things, with the light so bad you can barely pick me out if you don't know the sharp shape of my shoulders. One's out of focus even, me changing the sheets on my grandma's bed under the sloped thin roof I knock my head on when I sit up on the wrong side of the bed.

I try to look through the camera and see him and see what he saw, but all I see is the wood in his truck and that damned dog. I hear the dog, for sure, before I see him. That damned sorry dog, he was purebred something. Purebred dumb and noisy, kindly that. I never said it, though. That damn dog was whining and barking and jingling and, oh my God, the sound of his claws on my wide-board floors, digging out the new paint before the shine was even off. The only sound I relished that damned dog could make was the sound of his claws sliding in the back of the truck. Hardly that, though. More likely me plastered to the door with that damned dog drooling on my arm, yawning that high wheezy dog yawn, whining fit to kill.

Of course, there's not a picture anywhere of him or of that

damned dog. That was on purpose. There was one—I must have taken it with his camera. I can see it now as if I had it still. He has one of those cigarette-filtering things vise-gripped in his teeth with the dancing muscles in his jaw got still for once by the shot. His chin is so high you would think he was measuring a pine to slice it down. I'm glad he hunted the picture out, took it, probably burnt it. I don't want the damned thing.

I must have snapped the picture when we were cutting wood. He cut, I hauled and split. We must have cut six, seven face cords, maybe more, that summer. The splitting part was pure pleasure and precious little I got of that—maul up, straight up, then down with a clean split through the wood. My eyes didn't fail me once they learned, measured the perfect sweet spot in the log. I could split match sticks, I think, when my rhythm was right. Or that damned dog's skinny legs, for all that. I was sitting on that pile in those dozen pictures, slack-jawed and senseless, hands gripping the new-split logs. They were mine by then, the logs. The stacking twice, thrice, the splitting made them mine.

I told him that. I must have.

I kept the cords in the end and burned high roaring fires doused with kerosene. Log cabins, I built three logs high and three logs wide and torched them so they'd flash. That was later in the winter when the hundred degrees plus from can to can't was long gone, when I had real coffee back and not that damned instant he made me drink, when I had lipstick and a blue silk kimono and gold whore shoes on my feet.

The fires that summer were sure enough in the air, not kept in any firebox but flashing up with the slam of a truck door. I'd hear the yellow of the truck on the gravel road before I'd see the dust spumed up between the burnt-out rows of what used to be some crop. He'd come up the porch steps with that damned dog behind and we'd sit or lie somewhere where it was cooler yet, the kitchen floor maybe on the gray-painted boards with the fan sucking the hot around in eddies. That damned white slip or maybe the other stuff too would stick to my sweated skin before we went out to cut wood in the hundred degrees plus. Some days we wouldn't cut. Some days he'd sit on the porch in my sling-back chair and clinch his jaw until it looked like there were no bones at all, just muscles trebling up and down below his eyes. He'd read those notes out then. He would write them down before and read them off like some writ you would have served on you by the law. I can't remember what the words were—but when he finished he'd throw the scraps across the boards, across the tops of skittering blue-backed lizards come out to get themselves sunned.

Maybe that was later.

Maybe it was after the seven cords and the ironing board and the slant-sided ceiling above my Grandma's bed.

Have I said he mostly came and went? He'd whistle for that damned dog and put the chainsaw and the camera in the truck and the dust would billow at the bottom of my pine-strawed tracks and I'd take off the sticky slip and go back to my cooking or some other idling work. I can see sure enough from those pictures I didn't waste time at the mirror pencilling in my lips.

Sometimes he'd stay the night. But most days he'd go on home to air-conditioning and ice cream and television. Once or twice I went too when she was out of town—but mostly I liked the tree frogs and the pond across the road across the field and my broad-board floors underfoot to keep me cool and level.

Those nights with him there was always that damned dog whining and jingling and scratching something fierce and some-times, when he was getting going good, that damned dog would bark and then the whole thing would be a bust and I would turn off the light and try again in the dark, not speaking but trying to spread myself into more, so he had the feeling of the miles of his mother, not the razor-shouldered, sweat-grimed draggle that was me that sorry summer, the summer of the dog.

It was hot under the thin roof and even the gallon jar of tea didn't do much good. He blew on me—I remember that. I hauled the fan from room to room. The well water in the bath felt steamy. We piled up wood. I swung the maul and ironed—God knows what I ironed—it couldn't have been a dress.

Maybe it was the house itself and the spareness of it that brought that summer of the dog.

I didn't yet say that that damned dog chased the cat, chased it right out the second-story window, off my grandma's bed through the screen and into space. I fell down the slope of stairs, so scared I was that my heart was all I heard. The cat and I stayed resting there in the bushes, me mosquito-bit and sweated, the cat, his ears and whiskers moving, tracking dog. In the end, I wished I'd had his cat sense, although little enough it got him that day.

It was really just him and me that summer. I wasn't anybody's captive out there in my dog-trot house, but I stayed put. It wasn't like I waited for him, but he always came or sometimes he didn't. Usually in the afternoon he came. I guess he liked the habit of his days. I guess he liked me cooking dinner and the table set with candles. He'd sit quiet, no notes, no on and on about what should be.

In the morning I would wander. I'd loop the hills behind, trace the stream, lazy-like in the early part before the dapples marked the forest floor until such time I had to go and wait for that damned dog and him. I liked the house early like that, coming home with the sun barely up and the porch still cool or leastways not so flaming hot. I liked the two rooms up and two rooms down and the cat easy with no damned dog to fight. And then I'd hear the yellow and it would be the white slip or the firewood or the notes across the broad-board floor. What he used to say—by then he was mostly with me afternoons and some nights too—he used to say what was wrong with me, why I wasn't like the ones with television and ice cream, he'd list off those things, I can't remember what and tell me why I needed him and how I had erred before. He would write them down and read them off like something serious and official. I'd sit and measure out the field across the road, measure with my maul eye like it was waiting to be split from end to end. That damned dog would be laying there beside jingling and twitching and whining that high-pitched dog whine worse than any cat for sure or even any baby. Then after that we'd cut more wood or lay awhile inside.

It went along like that. Somewhere in there he took the pictures. Somewhere in there, he took his picture. His lists got longer. The burnt-out field split itself in two. The woodpile stopped rising to the sky right about when that hundred degrees plus was raised as hot as eight cords lit and burning fine, and the maul came down again and again.

I don't know why he took those pictures.

None there of me in the white slip or even splitting wood. He said to me, he said, "No one will ever love you like I do."

I didn't like that. It gave me a fright. He ripped out the shelves and such he built inside. He carted off nearly all that would fit in that yellow truck, that damned dog laying inside on the seat. I kept the wood, eight cords plus and burned it high and fast.

I think I see him still, in different places, different towns. I thought he trailed me as I walked one time. Anyway, he's right so far. I guess you never get what you didn't anyhow want. **Q**

Appendix

"How about here?" he asked, using his doctor voice, pressing his finger into my stomach. "Does it hurt here?" I said, "Yes, that's where it hurts. Yes," I said to him, "it hurts there," to each of the places that he pressed. I felt a burning where he touched, pain so sharp it made me want to clench my body around it. I said to him, "Dad, when you press it it really hurts. Do you have to press so hard? Even if you don't press so hard, I will still be able to tell you if it hurts." He said he was sorry but it was the procedure and pressed again, a little over to the side from the last place and just as hard. I said it hurt, and he kept pressing until after I said it hurt. So I started saying it hurt before it really did, so that when he kept on pressing it would really just be beginning to hurt. He pressed a few more places that hurt. Then he pressed another place, and I said it hurt. But when he kept on pressing, it did not hurt. He pressed again. I waited to see if it hurt. It did not, and I said to him, "Yes, that is where it hurts," and did he have to press so hard, that if he did not stop pressing so hard he was going to really hurt me. He stood up and said I would be all right. "No, I will not," I said. "It is burning up my insides," I said. "If you really tried, you would be able to feel it,"I said. But he just left the examination room—and that was the last time we touched. **Q**

ROBERT DOW

Little Nails

Why do I remember stripping off their clothes, getting her out of her panties and him out of his shorts, touching first his hard body, then hers with my fingers, putting my fingers everywhere there was to put them, spreading her legs, then taking the hammer and the nail and hammering the nail through him and into her Barbie, then laying them out? Ken on top, on the gold-tasseled, red satin pillow on my sister's bed, their tiny clothes, rolled up, torn, and strewn on the bedspread, Barbie's hair banged and tousled, her blue eyes open, looking nowhere, his new bent body cocked and driven into hers?

Why do I remember that when I finished I looked up to Him where He always was, hung, eyes shut, on the wall over her bed, the loincloth covering nothing that I could see, the crown of thorns painless, no wound in his side, the little nails nailed into His hands, into His tiny feet, and that then I reached down to them and pulled the nail slowly, painstakingly, from her body, not from Ken's, and that then, through him, nailed her a second time? **Q**

Gilbert and Sullivan

They sat at the bar, the actor's wife and the young man who had been given a small part in the last Fellini film. They sat, side by side, on seats of woven straw, drinking the white liqueur that tasted of licorice, the white liqueur all the Americans drank then because they thought it was the Italian's drink. They came, nearly every evening, at the end of the evening, to this same bar in one of the little side streets off the Via Veneto, where the big hotels were. It was where the Americans came to drink in those days, the movie people, and of all the bars they had made fashionable it was the most fashionable. They drank scotch here, or they drank gin. They drank vodka, and sometimes they drank three kinds of rum mixed with fruit juice. They came early, and ate a kind of cuisine concocted by a former chef from Polynesia. The Italians called it Chinese food because they thought that was what the Americans liked. But most of the time they came late, came after dining somewhere else, and drank the white liqueur out of big balloon glasses with coffee beans at the bottom.

Their eyes were filmed over, these Americans. They were bored, and their faces were curiously lacking in expression, but they were restless, too. Some of them worked regularly in the films. Some of them had names that had been known for a little while.

Some of them came and stayed, hoping to find roles. They stayed because it was cheap, and because they had left everything behind to come here, and so now there was nowhere else to go. This bar (Luau, it was called) had a sister of the same name in the place where they had come from. It had been started by two actors with a little money, and it had caught on, this Luau, because it made the movie people feel at home. Other people came, too, other Americans. They ate here, and they drank here, and they watched the movie people get into quarrels over practically nothing at all, or so it seemed to those who watched. The movie people drank and made fools of themselves, and the people who watched, the other Americans, liked that, liked watching the movie people misbehave for them.

"I hate this place," said the young man who had been given a small part in the last Fellini film.

"Do you?" said the actor's wife.

"Italians in Hawaiian shirts," said the young man who had gotten a small part in the last Fellini film.

"They only do it for the money," said the actor's wife.

"It is grotesque," said the young man who had gotten a small part in the last Fellini film.

"We come here," said the woman. "It is we who come here."

"Where else is there to go?" said the young man.

"The cherry trees are blooming in Kyoto," said the woman.

"Walter Devereaux's daughter," said the young man who had gotten a small part in the last Fellini film.

"Jack's picture was supposed to be finished last month," said the woman. "We will probably be here for another year."

"Nothing is happening back there," said the young man.

"Nothing is happening here, either," said the woman.

"I would like to be around when they start casting the new Fellini film," said the young man.

"They will not be casting for a couple of months," said the actor's wife. "Why not join Herbert in Spain for a while? They do not drink this stuff in Spain." The young man drank the rest of his drink, chewed on the coffee beans.

"I do not hear from Herbert," he said.

He smiled then, and he had a charming smile, the young man who had gotten a small part in the last Fellini film. He had the kind of smile that could make you change your mind about everything. You could just walk right into that smile, and she found herself responding to it, to his smile, the actor's wife, and she smiled back at him.

"Come on," said the young man, "let us go to the Pipistrella. Unless you are waiting for Jack. I did not ask if you were waiting for Jack. Are you waiting for Jack?"

In the Pipistrella, they sat at a small table angled into a corner, away from the music, and they sat there for a long time, drinking scotch and ordering ice, bowl after bowl of fresh ice, ordering ice because the Italians never gave enough ice and the Americans liked a lot of ice.

"I would like to get married," said the young man. "I think I would like to get married."

"Why would you want to do that?" said the woman.

"When I meet the girl, the sort of girl I want to meet, I will get married," said the young man

"Anyone can get married," said the woman. She indicated a fat woman, flame haired, and well over the age that was considered middle age, who was sitting at a table across the room with a pair of young Italians in tight suits.

"She could, for example, get married," said the woman.

"Hush," said the young man, grabbing her arm, capturing her hand in his hand and pressing it down against the table, looking around to see if anyone had noticed.

The woman pulled her arm away. She was very drunk now. She reached for the bottle of scotch, but the bottle was empty.

"I will bet you," said the woman. "I will bet you another bottle of scotch she could get married."

"Perhaps she already is," said the young man.

"The other one is her lover," said the woman.

The woman was aware that the young man had put his hand near her waist. She wondered whether or not to remove it, and decided instead to order a second bottle of scotch. She laughed and called for the waiter, but the waiter was serving another table and did not hear her call.

"Let us go now," said the young man. "We have been here too long. Come up to the apartment. I will give you a drink there."

So they left the Pipistrella, talking, laughing, and linking arms, as they strode up the street, rounded a corner, and mounted many flights of stairs to the apartment where the young man lived.

"What have you got to drink?" said the woman.

"Wine," said the young man. "Red wine, white wine, any kind of wine you like."

"Wine," said the woman.

"What about wine?" said the young man.

"I will use your bathroom," said the woman.

"Straight through the bedroom," said the young man. "You cannot miss it."

"You would be surprised," said the woman.

When the woman came out of the bathroom, the young man was lying on the bed in his dressing gown, smoking a cigarette. The woman sat down on the edge of the bed and took off her shoes. She reached over and took the young man's cigarette. She took a few puffs of the cigarette and gave it back to him.

"Where is my drink?" said the woman.

"Darling," said the young man.

"I want my drink in one of those big, Venetian-red glasses, hand-blown by the glassblowers of Venice. I want to look at you through Venetian-red glass.," said the woman.

The young man put out his cigarette and took the woman into his arms. They kissed.

"Where is my drink?"said the woman. "I want my drink."

He pulled her back another time.

"Leave me alone," she said.

He put his arm around her waist, drawing her back into his arms, back onto the bed, back into the sheets.

She shook him off, sat up, took a cigarette from the package on the night table, lit the cigarette, adjusted her clothes.

He lay back on the bed, his arm bent across his eyes. She touched the bottom of his foot. He turned onto his side, drew his knees up into his chest, pulled the robe tight around himself.

"It is cruel," he said.

"Oh, the actor's life for me," she said.

"Yes," he said.

"They say Gilbert drank," she said.

"Nothing will happen now," he said.

"Well," she said, "I guess that leaves Sullivan." **Q**

The Hollywood Babies Club

"Well," said the Hollywood Child, "here we are again."

"Dorothy Parker already said that," said the former debutante who played rich girls.

"In a story of the same name," said the fat daughter of the thin film star. "A long time ago."

"Before we were born," said her new husband.

"After we were born," said the fat daughter of the thin film star.

"Well," said the Hollywood Child, "I am saying it again. Walter always says there is nothing new under the sun. It is all in the marketing, Walter says."

"Walter?" said the new husband.

"Walter Devereaux," said the Hollywood Child. "My Father, of course."

"I did not know that," said the new husband. "I did not know you were Walter Devereaux's daughter."

"You are not a member of the club," said the Hollywood Child. "This is why you did not know."

"Of course he is a member," said the fat daughter of the thin film star. "He is my husband.'

"Husbands and wives are allowed to attend meetings. But they are not members," said the Hollywood Child.

"Says who?" said the comedian's son. "Says who?"

"Nobody can say anything," said the comedian's daughter. "We must vote on it."

"We cannot vote," said the Hollywood Child.

"Why not?" said the former debutante who played rich girls.

"Larry and Mark are not here," said the fat daughter of the thin film star. "I just noticed they're not."

"We cannot vote until everyone is here," said the new husband.

"Which brings me to another point," said the Hollywood Child. "Mark. Mark is another point."

"Mark?" said the director's son.

"Yes," said the Hollywood Child. "Mark. If husbands and wives are not members, then Mark cannot be a member."

"Larry and Mark are always together," said the comedian's son. "You always see them like that, together."

"They are never apart," said the comedian's daughter.

"They are together more than husbands and wives," said the former debutante.

"But they are not husband and wife," said the fat daughter of the thin film star.

"They are less than husband and wife," said the new husband.

"No," said the Hollywood Child. "They are more."

"She is right," said the director's son. "It is more difficult to find a Mark than to find a husband or to find a wife."

"You always back her up, Ruben," said the former debutante who played rich girls.

"They were brought up together," said the fat daughter of the thin film star. "They were never apart."

"Like Larry and Mark," said the new husband.

"Walter Devereaux's daughter and Ruben Costigan's son," said the former debutante who played rich girls.

"Let us stop this bickering and have another drink," said the comedian's son.

"Let us go into the Christmas Tree Room and have more drinks," said the comedian's daughter. "I am tired of this room. The Christmas Tree Room will put us into a better mood."

"That is a good idea," said the Hollywood Child. "We cannot vote until Larry and Mark are here."

"God!" said the Hollywood Child, as the group followed the comedian's children into another room. "I cannot believe that Christmas tree."

"He keeps it up all year," said the comedian's son.

"We are not allowed to touch it," said the comedian's daughter. "We are not allowed to do it."

"The ornaments must be filthy," said the fat daughter of the thin film star. "Just perfectly filthy."

"The servants clean them," said the comedian's son.

"Only Margaret," said the comedian's daughter. "Margaret is the only one who is allowed to touch that tree."

"Are there presents under it at Christmas?" said the Hollywood Child. "Tell me if there are."

"We do not give Christmas presents," said the comedian's son.

"We do not get Christmas presents," said the comedian's daughter. "It's not done."

"You have never received Christmas presents?" said the director's son. "You never got any?"

"He stopped all that a long time ago," said the comedian's son.

The comedian's daughter pressed a buzzer. Everyone waited. Nothing happened.

"Where is Frank?" said the comedian's son.

"You know," said the comedian's daughter.

A handsome young man with tousled hair and a rumpled smoking jacket appeared.

"What do you want, Gloria?" said the handsome young man.

"We want some more drinks," said the comedian's daughter.

"And Frank," said the comedian's son, "do not be all day about it. We want the drinks now."

"In a minute," said the handsome young man. "I have to take care of upstairs first."

"Upstairs?" said the Hollywood Child when the handsome young man with the tousled hair and the rumpled smoking jacket had left the room.

"You know," said the comedian's son.

"Mother," said the comedian's daughter.

"Who was that?" said the new husband.

"That was Frank," said the fat daughter of the thin film star.

"Frank?" said the new husband.

"The butler," said the Hollywood Child.

"The butler?" said the new husband.

"Yes," said the director's son. "Frank is the butler."

The doorbell rang. It rang for a long time, playing the opening bars of "White Christmas" as it rang.

"Larry and Mark," said the former debutante who played rich girls. "It's Larry and Mark."

"I will answer the door," said the comedian's daughter.

"I will mix more drinks," said the comedian's son.

"Good idea," said the comedian's daughter. "One never knows how long Frank will be."

In the Christmas Tree Room, the comedian's son freshened everyone's drinks. The comedian's daughter returned with two young men. The young men wore matching bellhop jackets trimmed with gold braid.

"Here are Larry and Mark," said the comedian's daughter.

"Hello, Larry and Mark," said the comedian's son.

"Yes," said the director's son, "now we can vote."

"I have a bone to pick with you," said one of the young men.

"Larry has a bone to pick with you," said one of the young men. "Larry has a real bone to pick."

"Which bone would that be?" said the comedian's son.

"I will tell you if you buy me a drink," said the first young man. "And not until you buy me one."

"Larry needs a drink," said the second young man.

The comedian's son went to the bar and mixed a drink for the first young man. The comedian's son did not mix a drink for the second young man.

"What about Mark?" said the new husband.

"Mark does not drink, you idiot!" said the Hollywood Child.

"How snappish we are," said the fat daughter of the thin film star. "My, my, how very snappish."

The first young man drank half his drink and set it down on a bombé chest, making a large, wet ring on the chest.

"I have a bone to pick with you," said the first young man a second time. "No kidding, I really do."

"Larry has a bone to pick with you," said the second young man. "Larry really has one."

"What bone do you have to pick?" said the comedian's son.

"Yes," said the comedian's daughter, "what is the bone you have to pick with us?"

"It is that song your doorbell is playing," said the first young man. "You know that song?"

"The doorbell is playing 'White Christmas,'" said the comedian's son. "Don't you know 'White Christmas?'"

"I know it is playing 'White Christmas,'" said the first young man. "That is the point."

"What is the point?" said the comedian's daughter.

"I am tired of 'White Christmas,'" said the first young man. "It is all I ever hear. You could do a friend a favor and have your doorbell play the other Christmas song."

"Larry wants you to play the other Christmas song," said the second young man.

"What difference does it make?" said the director's son.

"If you were Larry, it would make a difference," said the former debutante who played rich girls.

"All Christmas songs are banal," said the Hollywood Child.

"Why are we talking about Christmas?" said the fat daughter of the thin film star.

"Yes," said the new husband. "Why are you talking about Christmas? Christmas is months away."

"Are you sure?" said the comedian's son.

"I thought it was Christmas," said the comedian's daughter. "I really thought it was."

"It must be Christmas," said the director's son. "The Christmas tree is up. That's why it must be."

"The Christmas tree is always up," said the Hollywood Child.

"They never take the Christmas tree down in this house," the former debutante who played rich girls said.

"I am not interested in Christmas," said the first young man, "but I wish you would play the other Christmas song."

"Larry wants you to play the other Christmas song," said the second young man. "It's the one Larry wants."

"Let us vote," said the Hollywood Child. "We have wasted enough time. It's time to vote."

"Just a minute," said the fat daughter of the thin film star. "I want to get something straight."

"Yes," said the new husband, "Let us straighten this Christmas thing out before we vote."

"What Christmas thing?" said the Hollywood Child. "I fail to see the issue."

"The issue is whether or not it is Christmas," said the former debutante who played rich girls. "You see the issue?"

"And the fact that the Christmas tree is up is irrelevant in this instance," said the Hollywood Child.

"Certainly it is Christmas," said the comedian's son. "There are presents under the tree. We never have presents."

"So obviously it is Christmas," said the comedian's daughter.

"But you never have presents," said the former debutante who played rich girls. "Presents do not prove anything one way or another. They actually don't."

"When we were little, we used to have presents," said the comedian's son.

"Perhaps he has decided to go back to presents," said the comedian's daughter. "Perhaps this has been his decision."

"It is not Christmas," said the fat daughter of the thin film star.

"It is the Fourth of July," said the new husband, who was not accustomed to the number of drinks he had consumed.

"Shall we vote on it?" said the Hollywood Child.

"Let us vote on it," said the director's son.

The butler appeared in the doorway. He slicked back his tousled hair and adjusted his rumpled smoking jacket. "Drinks, anyone?" said the butler.

"Ah," said the comedian's son, "here is Frank. Maybe he can help us. Can you help us, Frank?"

"Yes," said the comedian's daughter. "It is the sort of thing Frank would know."

"Frank," said the Hollywood Child and the director's son, "we all want to know whether or not it is Christmas."

"It is not Christmas," said the fat daughter of the thin film star. "Tell them, Frank. Would you please tell them?"

"It is the Fourth of July," said the new husband. "Am I right, Frank? Tell them I am right."

"It is not Christmas," said the butler.

"If it is not Christmas, then why are there Christmas presents under the tree?" said the comedian's son.

"There are always Christmas presents under the tree," said the butler. "There never are not presents there."

"There are?" said the comedian's daughter. "I do not remember ever seeing them."

"That is probably because you have never not seen them," said the Hollywood Child.

"I told you that it was not Christmas," said the fat daughter of the thin film star.

"It is the Fourth of July," said the new husband.

"No," said the butler. "It is not the Fourth of July."

"Then what is it?" said the director's son.

"Yes," said the Hollywood Child. "What is it?"

"I do not know," said the butler.

"You do not know?" said the comedian's son.

"No," said the butler. "I do not know what day it is." **Q**

The Red Raincoat

She sat there, the woman in the red raincoat, sat there at the very back, with her friend and her friend's husband. They were surrounded by poor people. No one spoke the language she spoke. Everyone wore raincoats. There were no other Americans sitting on the benches. The husband of the woman's friend had a cold. He coughed occasionally. Once, he sneezed into a large, white handkerchief. Some of the other people on the benches coughed. Several of them sneezed. None of the others had large, white handkerchiefs. No one spoke. Everyone waited. A man sat holding a radio, shiny black, that played that music.

"What is happening?" said the woman in the red raincoat.

"It is a good sign," said her friend.

"I think something has happened," the woman said. "It is taking too long."

"If anything had happened, Howard would have come out. immediately."

"It is taking too long," said the woman.

"It is just the opposite," said her friend. "When something happens they come out right away."

The husband sneezed again into his handkerchief.

"Plop! Plop! Fizz! Fizz!" said a child.

"How do you know that?" said the woman.

"It stands to reason," said her friend. "If you think about it carefully you will realize that I am right. You will realize it is the only logical explanation, if you think about it carefully."

"Everything is logical," said the woman.

"No," said her friend. "It is a good sign."

The husband coughed. The man turned up his radio.

"Plop! Plop! Fizz! Fizz!" said a child.

"Look," the woman said. "It is Howard. He has come out from the back. He wants us to go up there to the front."

"I will come with you," said her friend. "Jerry and I will come with you. We will all go."

The woman in the red raincoat got up and went to the front of the room. The man, Howard, came to meet her. He put his arm around her shoulders, sheltering her from her friends. "They got him back once," said Howard, "but they lost him again."

"They got him back?" said the woman.

"Once," the man, Howard, said. "But they lost him again."

"Will they get him back a second time?" said the woman.

"Perhaps," said Howard. "They might perhaps do it. But," said Howard, "he will be of no use to you, will he?" **Q**

Watson's Boy

HIS KEYS

He carries two hundred and thirty-five rings of keys. His father has constructed harnesses for him to loop over his arms, chest, and waist, upon which the keys hang. The harnesses consist of heavy canvas straps, oversewn and strung with hooks.

When he walks, the keys rattle upon his flesh, making his skin tingle. He tries the keys in the locks. The keys do not seem to fit the locks. He continues on, to other doors.

It once gave Brey particular satisfaction to run through dark hallways, the keys sounding against his body. Now he does not run, but lumbers. The increasing weight of keys stunts his movement, cripples his growth. He does not resent this—he does not realize it. According to his father's calculations, when Brey gathers five hundred keys the load will become too heavy. His spine will snap. His father suggests that he should stop at four hundred, and for that reason has equipped the harness with only four hundred hooks. Brey, however, has realized that each hook can be bent to hold two rings of keys. If he continues to collect keys, Brey will someday find himself lying on the ground with a broken back, calling for his father quietly, as if embarrassed.

The keys seem to be as regular a fixture of the halls as the doors. They are covered with dust where the halls are dusty. They are free from dust where the halls are clean.

He does not know if the halls will continue to exist when all the keys are removed from their intersections. He experiments to discover if, once the keys are gone, the halls will disappear. Perhaps, he believes, they will vanish from around him, allowing him an infinitely accessible space.

The discovery of a set of keys invokes in him a series of gestures. He picks up the keys. He examines them, assures himself that they resemble the other keys he has found. He hangs the keys from a hook of his harness, then returns to his rooms, trying the new keys in the familiar doors.

If keys exist, doors must exist which they will unlock. Such is the nature of the key. Such is the nature of the door.

He has traveled through two hundred and thirty-six intersections and in the center of each has found keys. He does not know how many intersections exist. He has reached one outer, terminal wall, beyond which he cannot progress. For this reason, he suspects that the halls are not infinite.

His father thinks differently. "Everything is a passage," he says, "though not every passage leads somewhere."

His father has never been wrong. Brey tries to push his way through the terminal wall. The wall seems solid, essential in every regard. His fingers find no passage. He gives up.

His father instills within Brey his respect for keys. His father tells him:

"The keys are in the hallways, at every intersection. I have never collected keys. If you collect them, I will be pleased. If you choose not to collect them, I will not question your choice."

HIS HALLWAYS

The floors of his halls are polished black stone. The walls are rough, dark stone, as are the ceilings. His hallways are extensive, forming perfect grids. Each hall between the intersections has ten doors upon each side. Each door is distanced from the next by two spans of Brey's arms—one and one half spans of his father's arms. The halls are lit by light bulbs hanging single and naked over the intersections. The bulbs are of various wattage, and expire periodically. In certain intersections, the halls are nearly dark, lit only by light bulbs four intersections distant. In other intersections, the halls are brightly lit, the polished floors glistening as if wet. There, the light bulbs are globes, larger than he imagines his brain to be.

The terminal wall is different. On the terminal wall, there are only doors on the inner side of the hall. On the outer side, in the place of doors, windows have been cut into the stone. The windows are filled with glass. The glass is black, opaque, but shiny enough that in it Brey sees his own ghost.

The hall ahead grows dark, the light bulb broken or missing. Brey travels by touch through the dim, unreeling his fishline. He has always been afraid of the dark. He counts ten doors, feels the wall sheer off before him.

He sets the reel of fishline aside. He eases down to his knees, sweeps his hands forward across the floor until they brush something. He fumbles a ring of keys from the floor, ticks off the keys upon it. There are seven keys. This is true of all rings of keys, an essential quality of rings of keys.

He returns, following the fishline back to the tenth door. He wraps the fishline around the handle of the door, sets the reel down on the ground. He follows the fishline backward, stopping before each door to try each of his seven keys in the lock.

The walls are rough. He uses them to scrape the dead skin from his elbows. He has not discovered either graft or joint in the wall. To Brey, the walls seem to be carved from a single block of stone. Perhaps his father would disagree.

The floors are smooth. Echoes rise from the soles of his boots. The walls and floor might be carved from the same stone, though the one is polished while the other is not. Why one might be polished and the other not, Brey cannot guess. For him, they may as well be different types of stone.

Brey was born in the halls, as was Brey's father. What occupied the halls before them, Brey cannot say. If Brey's father knows, he keeps it a secret, perhaps for Brey's own good. If his father knew and if it were important, Brey knows his father would tell him. Brey does not need to know.

THE DOORS IN THE HALL

The doors in his halls are all locked. They seem to him identical. He has measured himself against the doors. The doorways are large enough to admit him, but little larger. There is a handsbreadth of space to either side of his shoulders, two handsbreadths above his head. His father, on the other hand, must stoop to fit within the door-frame.

The doors are made of unvarnished wood. Four of the doors are unlocked. All of the other doors are locked. Excepting the bedroom door, the doors which are unlocked hinge inward. The hinges lie hidden, cradled in stone.

He feels his way along the dark hallway. He stops to lean against the wall. He disentangles the fishline from around the door handle, heaves up the reel.

He carries the reel with both hands, resting it against his thighs. The weight of it digs the keys into his legs. He travels forward, unspooling the fishline.

He drops the reel. He kicks the keys out of the intersection, nearer to the wall. He braces his body against the wall, squats down, steadying one hand upon the reel. He takes the keys from the floor. In standing, as his father has taught him, he looks up at the ceiling. The purpose of this, Brey does not know.

Sick, Brey feels the weight of the keys. The hallways are cold. He drags his shoulders and face along the wall, shivering.

He drags his face too heavily. His skin abrades, breaks, bleeds, the old scars splitting back.

Brey would be handsome, but his face is scarred. He would be handsome had not his growth been stumped by the keys. Brey would be handsome, if the word had any significance for him.

Brey's father never carried keys. His face once was smooth. He was gathered up to a colossal height.

Now he is old. His face is puckered and wrinkled. His back is stooped. But he is still taller than Brey.

Brey turns accidental circles in the dark hallways, reversing his course. He reaches a previous intersection whose keys he has removed He leans against the wall, catching his breath.

He feels the floor for keys. He finds nothing.

He keeps stooping, keeps searching.

"Father?" he yells, "Father?"

He carries three hundred and fifty-seven pounds of keys upon his body. If he falls to the ground, he will find it difficult to rise. If he is injured in the fall, he will lie upon the ground until he starves or until he thinks to remove the keys so as to stand.

He stumbles forward across the intersection, strikes the opposite wall. Leaning against the wall, he moves forward. He counts doors as he passes them, continuing toward new intersections.

Of doors, there are two possibilities. Perhaps the doors were made at the same time as the halls. Perhaps the doors were cut later. There is no evidence to allow Brey to favor either one hypothesis or the other. But he prefers the former.

BREY'S ROOM

The frame of his bed stands beside the door. His body is too heavy for it. Next to it is spread a pallet. He sleeps upon the pallet in clothes and keys, adjacent to the frame.

His bed frame rises into a rickety canopy. Shredded fabric hangs from it, seemingly held together by cobwebs and dust.

On the opposite side of the room are a broken chair, a desk, and several notebooks. Each notebook begins with a single map of the hallways which he has explored. Following are scores of theoretical maps, numerous postulated sets of hallways.

His walls are bare. In the ceiling is a bank of twelve light bulbs, cradled in a depression of stone, bulbs abutted one to another. Five of the light bulbs have failed, two during Brey's lifetime. Brey will never forget the drama of those moments. The remaining light bulbs stay lit while Brey is awake, switching off when he lays down to sleep. The mechanism that regulates the light remains obscure to him.

Attached to the desk is a strand of fishline which wraps around the leg of the desk four times before being tied off. The line runs out under the door, down the hall, through empty intersections, toward the terminal wall. The line is neither taut nor loose.

He sits cross-legged upon his pallet, poring over his maps. All the maps partake of the same design, making it difficult to distinguish one map from another. If Brey's imagined maps were not clearly marked, he would find it difficult to distinguish them from his real map.

His imaginary maps contain imaginary keys in each intersection. All maps are gridwork. All are recorded on equally sized sheets of squared paper. The only difference between them is where Brey marks the location of the terminal doors.

The terminal doors are recorded on the imagined maps but have not yet been discovered in the hallways. The terminal doors exist on terminal walls, breaking the succession of blacked windows. The terminal doors stretch to the ceiling. They are two large, varnished doors, locked. No light departs through their bottom crack. Some little light comes through the locks, outlining them, suggesting that something exists beyond. An eye to the keyhole, Brey believes, would reveal only an elaborate gearage.

The terminal doors must lead out of the halls. Otherwise, Brey would not call them "terminal."

Perhaps through the terminal doors lies another set of hallways, organized according to principles of which his own halls are merely a shadow. The terminal doors exist: They have been discovered on all maps, excepting the actual map. Thus, they must eventually be discovered on the actual map. Thus, reasons Brey, they must be discovered in the halls themselves.

Before he collects all the keys, he hopes to find the terminal doors. When he finds them, he will attempt to escape.

Perhaps the terminal doors are hidden in a dark section of hallway. Perhaps he has walked by them, pressed against the opposite wall, again and again, unaware.

He returns to his room to find his room open, his father standing over his desk, thumbing through his map books.

"Brey, will you explain what these are?" says his father.

"Notebooks?" says Brey.

"You know what I mean," says his father

"Maps?" says Brey.

"Maps?" says his father, crumpling them. "Maps of what, Brey? These are useless."

HIS PARENTS

His parents live in the room adjacent to his own. They are withered of skin, but not of mind. They are the source of all his knowledge. His mother never leaves the room. His father rarely is to be found in the room. He wanders.

Brey has wrapped his mother's body with strips of sheets to protect her from rats. He has done this at his father's request. Brey has never seen rats. He has read about them at length, and has learned about them from his father. His father wanders the halls looking for evidence of the rats.

"The rats," his father confides, "exist! I have seen them, Brey. Someday they will return to these halls."

Brey has not seen the rats. He has seen drawings of rats in his father's books about rats. He believes in the rats, though he has not seen them. He trusts his father.

"Your mother and I have killed rats," says his father. "Someday they will return for me or for your mother. I am still capable of running from them. Your mother is not. If she is disguised in sheets, however, they might pass her by."

If the rats do discover Brey's mother, they might find it difficult to chew through her wrappings. It might take them long enough to chew through the sheets that they would choose instead to search out other bodies. Brey's body, for example, or that of his father. Brey's father can run from the rats. Brey can lumber from them. If he is not fast enough to escape, his keys might still protect him. Even if the rats chew through his mother's sheets, they will chew through at only one spot. The rats will stream into his mother through the single hole, eating the body hollow. If Brey surprises the rats, he will be able to sew the hole shut. The rats will be trapped. They will suffocate within his mother.

No one shall wrap Brey in sheets when he grows feeble. There is nobody to do it. He will be easy prey to rats.

When he approaches death, he will hang himself from one of the light fixtures in the hallway, out of reach of the rats. Perhaps he will collect enough keys that his entire body will be covered, armored against rats. A smart rat, however, will snout past the keys.

The wrapped feet of Brey's mother hang over the edge of her bed. His mother says little, almost never speaking directly to Brey. His father claims, however, that she asks about him often. That she is concerned about him.

His father tells him things about keys, about halls, nothing else. His father says this of the keys: "There are two ways to get the keys: you can collect the keys or you can wait for them to collect you. I have done the latter. The keys have not come. I have no regrets—there are things more important than keys."

HIS KNOWLEDGE

His mother tells him little about herself. He knows that she has always been in these halls, little more. His father is modest, speaking seldom of his own accomplishments. He knows of his father no more than he can gather from his father's commentary on rats, halls, keys. There are only stories of rats, elaborate rat traps, his father's refusal to collect keys: "If I had it to do again, I would change nothing. I do not believe in regret. Nevertheless, I wonder if you should reconsider your own course."

His knowledge of his father lies in his father's drawings and poems. His father has mentioned thousands of drawings, of rats. Brey has found only a single sheet of paper with two ink drawings upon it, plastered underneath the sink. The lines are faint, but the shapes of rats are still trapped there.

Often, Brey himself traces rats on the table with his fingers. In this, he considers himself his father's child.

He has torn pages from his notebook and drawn pictures of rats upon them, leaving them scattered through the intersections for his father to find. The drawings have disappeared, but his father has never said anything about them. Perhaps the drawings are good enough that Brey's father thinks they are his own. Perhaps the rats find them first, destroying them.

His father's poems are in a slim volume labeled "To My Darling Brey: He Has Chosen to Collect Keys." His father has said nothing to Brey of the book's existence. Brey discovered it in his parents' room while his father was wandering, his mother asleep. The book was wedged between the headboard and the wall. He slid the book from its hiding place, apparently without his mother and father's knowledge, and conveyed it into his room to hide under his pallet. At times, as he sleeps, he feels the shape of it beneath him. His father has never noted its absence.

There are forty-six poems in the book. Brey knows they are poems because below each title is written the words "A Poem." Since he has stolen the book, Brey does not dare discuss the poems with his father. The poems are about rats. None of the poems scan. None rhyme. Nonetheless, Brey is moved. He is secretly proud of his father and of what the man has done.

The halls contain myriad sounds. He has the sounds of his boots in the halls, the echo of his fists upon the windows, the jangle of his keys, the drip of his water, the hum of his light bulbs, the sound of his father's footsteps, fading. When a light bulb expires, the light sputters and offers an ecstatic sound, much rarer. Then a hall falls dark, silent.

At times there is the sound of his father's voice in the halls. In the past, his mother's voice as well. Now his mother's voice does not leave its room.

His father never says: "I have written poems, and this is what they mean."

His father says, "Brey, I am not here for your benefit. I am your father, but I am other things besides a father. I will help you as I can, but I will not sacrifice myself to you."

His father says, "Do you think collecting keys is the best choice for you, Brey?"

HIS KITCHEN
His kitchen is a room paneled in white plastic, panels

stretching from ceiling to floor. Where two panels meet, a metal strip covers the crack. The walls, when soiled, can be wiped clean with damp cloth.

Each sheet of the wall hides a pantry. To reveal the pantry, one must grasp the metal strip at a designated point, pulling outward. The pantries are expansive. There has always been enough food for Brey and for his parents.

His father says of the stove in one of his poems, "Once it was a great truth." What this means, Brey does not pretend to know. He is not privy to the truths of a stove.

The faucet handles of the sink have sheared off, but the gaskets remain relatively intact. Water drips slowly from the cracked spigot. Beneath the spigot, Brey has placed a pewter cup. When it fills with water, he pours it into a canteen.

It takes several hours for the cup to fill. As his journeys through the halls become lengthier, the cup sometimes overflows and water is lost. He collects a cup of water when he leaves to walk the halls, a cup when he returns to sleep. He does not know if his father and mother drink from his cup while he is gone. Brey is not dying of thirst by any means, yet he is often thirsty.

There is a table in the kitchen. Under the table is a paper sack. When the sack is full of garbage, Brey surreptitiously dumps it into one of the hallways

On the table are stacked four books: *The Rat*, *Rats: All About Them*, *Our Friend the Rat*, and *How to Build a Better Mousetrap*. His father's name has been written inside each front cover, though Brey has had the books for as long as he can remember.

Brey has read these books, studying the pictures carefully. He knows the rat. He is prepared.

HIS TILES

The floor of the bathroom is covered with thousands of identical square tiles. Brey has transformed this floor into a map, placing scraps of cardboard at the intersections of the tiles. He has found one hundred and twelve sets of keys travelling to the terminal wall, one hundred and twenty-nine more traveling along the terminal wall. Assuming that the halls form a quadrangle, there are a minimum of fourteen thousand four hundred and forty-eight sets of keys in the halls. Of these he can expect to collect five hundred—approximately three and one-half percent.

He wets his finger in the bowl of the toilet, rubs it against his skin. Dirt and dead skin flake away. His father continues to warn him against using the toilet in this fashion. "Sanitation, son, is not a game." Brey sees no alternative.

HIS WINDOWS AND WALLS

His windows line the terminal walls. They are textureless, black, opaque. He has tried to scrape their darkness away with his keys. The keys slip from the glass.

He pounds on the glass with both fists. When he strikes the glass, it vibrates. The vibration is not unlike the sound of his boots as they strike the floor.

He presses his ear against the glass. He hears nothing.

Brey has seen pictures of windows in his rat books. He has seen windows with rats nestling upon their sills. He knows the purpose of windows. They are for rats to look through, a sort of transparent wall. When rats tire, they draw drapes.

He raises his hands to pound on the windows. He feels a hand on his shoulder. He lets his hands fall.

"Brey?" says his father. "Do you think that is wise?"

"Wise?" says Brey.

"Do you wish to attract rats?"

"Rats?" says Brey.

"Are you ready for them?" says his father. "Are you prepared? Brey?" he says. "Brey?"

HIS FISHLINE

The fishline was the gift of his father. It is wound around a wheel-rimmed spool as thick as Brey's torso. The words "#20-Test Premium Fishline: 21,120 feet (approx. four miles)" are stenciled on both wheels of the spool.

Brey does not know what "miles" are. He has never heard nor seen the word "feet" used in this sense before.

His father explains. "It is called fishline because it is fishline."

His father volunteers nothing more about fishline, only informing Brey that it is fishline. Brey masters this information, makes it his own.

He takes a ring of keys off his belt. Opening the ring's gate, he slips the fishline inside the ring. He hooks the ring back onto his waist.

The fishline whirs past him as he walks, slipping through the eye of the ring, a hiss beneath the clank of keys.

He walks down the halls toward the next set of keys. He picks away a half-scabbed cut on one hand, lengthening it, deepening it. He stops to rinse his hand with water from the canteen. The water drips onto the polished floor, separating into beads. Holding aside the keys that cover his shirt, he presses his hand against the fabric. He wipes the hand dry.

He passes empty intersections, enters dark halls. Light returns, then fades. He trusts to the fishline.

He reaches the last explored intersection. There is his father.

"Hello, Brey," his father says.

He and Brey shake hands.

"Are you sure that collecting keys is the right choice?" says his father. "Are you prepared for every contingency?"

Brey nods, passes through the intersection. Beyond, the halls grow brighter still. He approaches the next intersection.

He hesitates, halts. Allows his eyes to adjust.

The intersection is heaped ankle-deep with dust. No keys are visible. Brey hesitates. He turns away. The intersection behind him is empty, his father gone. **Q**

Monsters

Counting this time—and she is counting—Sheba has held the animal twice in her arms. The animal is not one of her belongings, but her sister is.

This is a woman's story. None of the men will like this.

Sheba has been returned from Munich where she stayed at the Arabella Westpark Hotel at Garmisher Strasse 2. At the Heimeranplatz S-bahn station, she has been rescued from considerable danger by Denis. He was in Munich on business, coincidentally. Denis had to let go an employee in Munich. Denis had to be a beast. In Munich, he didn't want to be.

Now, at 4 Rue Cassette in Paris, Denis is in his home, with Sheba, and the cat, and the furniture. Denis appears to be suffering, has on his overcoat indoors. He raps on the chair on which Sheba sits with the cat and he says, "Why are you like this?" The cat is sphinx-like. Denis pauses to consider how any monster may have poise, originality, and charm, and occasionally enjoy a foray to an almost unforgettable, dismal end.

That's when Sheba lets go. The cat makes a choice about what to do next, and the other two are inclined to. **Q**

Diagnosis

All this business, it is such a relief, she thought, when she did stop to think, but when she did not stop to think, she felt heart-breaking cramping.

There is no evidence yet on his condition.

She stretched her arms out over her head. She was woozy, so that she might not have seen the cold light of day.

"You were right about nearly everything," she said. It was a shot in the dark.

"About what?" he asked her.

Hearing that, she really shot him with her real gun.

Unable to get a direct flight to safe haven, she had to pass through New York. In New York, her torn ligament was diagnosed and her leg was put into a cast.

And then, during one of his emotional outbursts, the chief hospital physician informed her that she also suffered from the effects of a massive myocardial infarct, as well as, chronic uveitis, irreversible glaucoma, and thyreotoxicosis. **Q**

DIANE WILLIAMS

The Capture

It is cubed. It has to be good. She displays the cheese in glass bowls. The stewing chickens—they didn't lay eggs, and they got their heads chopped off. They are tough. The fryer, the Purdue, the capon—they are tender is her verdict on them.

She sees the time of the day on the clock on her wall. For herself, she takes this advice: Ponder large answerable questions. Believe believable things. Her table is set. Pursuit and revenge are her plan. She is at her own table in the presence of herself. Now she is eternally there because of what I have said about her here. She is being restrained for her remainder. She is my conscience. **Q**

A Place

I am on the train, heading home, when I notice the story in the newspaper. It seems there has been another murder. The man had been my age, but unmarried. He'd been beaten with baseball bats by thugs on the loose. Along with the story, there is a photograph of the crime scene. It seems unusually stark and colorless. It shows blood but no body.

"So, how are things?"

I turn to face a man I'd noticed some time before, standing alone at the other end of the car. He is taller than I am. He has a briefcase wedged up under one arm. He offers me a cigarette, and I take it, though I believe my wife thinks I've quit.

"Things aren't so good," I say, putting down the paper. "There are many problems."

"At home? At work?" he says.

I nod my head and watch him light my cigarette.

"At work, yes," I say. "There are problems at work."

He lights his own cigarette, then looks at me as if he wants me to go on.

I say, "You see, the thing is, I've been sleeping with my supervisor's wife."

"Ah," the man says. "And your supervisor has found out about it, is that it?"

"I don't know," I say. "If he has, he doesn't seem to mind. He's always smiling at me now, and touching his hand to my shoulder as if he wants us to be friends. The other thing is, he keeps promoting me—three promotions in the past three months."

"Well, he must like you," the man says.

"Yes, but I distrust him," I say.

"Yes, of course, I understand," the man says.

"And it's strange," I say. "My supervisor is a very attractive man. Did I mention this already?"

"No," the man says.

"Well, he is," I say. "And here I am sleeping with his wife."

"Is the wife attractive?" the man says.

I say, "I suppose someone might think so. I mean, there's nothing terribly wrong with her. She's not disfigured in any way."

The man says, "But you yourself don't find her particularly attractive, do you?"

"Me myself?" I say. "No. Not particularly."

"Yet you're sleeping with her," the man says.

"Yes," I say.

I stare at my cigarette.

"I guess I don't understand," the man says, gently, after a while. "Why do it if you're not attracted to her?"

"Well," I say, looking at him, "we have to do it, don't we?"

"I'm afraid I don't follow you," the man says.

I say, "Men, I mean. We have to sleep with women. We have no choice. It's strictly biological."

"Only if you believe the biologists," the man says.

He says this quietly, then takes a long, slow pull from his cigarette. It occurs to me that he is holding his cigarette in a rather unusual way. As perhaps an actor would. As if he is aware of other people being aware of how he holds his cigarette.

"Are you married?" the man asks me.

"Well, of course. I'm the age for it," I say

"Me, too," the man says.

"Married?" I ask.

He looks at me and smiles.

"Well, of course. I'm that age," the man says.

He takes another pull from his cigarette. I find myself liking this man. He has blue eyes. When he smiles, they twinkle.

Then he says, "Have you ever killed a man?"

The question startles me a little, coming out of the blue as it does. I notice that he is staring at me, and not smiling at all anymore. For the first time, I notice that he is sweating, that he has probably been sweating all along, that there are tiny beads of sweat on his forehead and under his nose.

"Well, yes, of course," I say. "I killed men in the war. Didn't you kill men? In the war?"

The man shakes his head, looks down at the floor.

He says, "It's because of my feet, you see."

"Oh," I say. I look at his feet. In shoes, they look normal enough. "That's too bad," I say.

"I don't know," the man says, looking out the windows of the train. "I guess I've never had a great desire."

"Desire?" I say.

The man says, "To kill, I mean."

"Well, no, of course not," I say. "But it was never a matter of desire. It was war. We were given guns. The enemy was described to us. It was made clear they had committed atrocities."

"So you had no choice," the man says.

"Well, no, of course not. But it's not choice that matters, now is it?" I say. "It's whatever it takes to get from day to day."

The man says, "Yes. Day to day. That makes sense to me."

He looks out the windows of the train.

"So," I say, trying to change the subject, "how are things with you?"

"Things aren't so good," the man says. "I have purchased a weapon. I have it here in my briefcase." I watch him push the briefcase up tighter under his arm.

"Ah," I say. "For protection."

The man shakes his head.

"It's because of all these thoughts I've been having lately," the man says.

"About all the crime," I say. "Yes, of course. There's a story in the paper today." I hold up the newspaper for him to see.

"I've been having all these thoughts about my wife."

I put the paper down. I suddenly feel in error for showing it to him. It is wrong to give people ideas about such things.

"You mean you've been thinking about killing your wife?"

The man looks at me, then looks away, out the windows of the train. I find myself wondering what he's looking for out there. "You must think I'm insane," the man says.

I have the sudden desire to touch my hand to his shoulder.

"I know what it means to have a wife," I say.

The man says, "She's just always seemed so different to me."

"Women are," I say.

"Yet we marry them," the man says.

"We have no choice," I say.

"It's biological," the man says.

"Yes," I say.

We stand in silence for a while, not smoking any more, just standing in silence, comfortable with each other, not at all as it's supposed to be when you are standing among strangers.

Finally, the man says, "Why don't you tell me something about your wife. Is she attractive?"

I try to picture my wife, but in my mind she cannot be summoned. I remember only that her eyes are not blue.

"I suppose there is nothing terribly wrong with her," I say.

The man nods his head, understanding.

"And your wife?" I say. "Is she attractive?"

I watch the man think about this for a while. Then he looks at me, his eyes twinkling.

He says, "She's not disfigured in any way."

We smile at each other, very quickly, then go back to smoking our cigarettes. After a while, I feel the train slowing to a stop.

"Well," the man says, dropping his cigarette onto the floor, "this is as far as I go."

"Oh," I say, looking out the windows of the train. "You live around here, do you?"

"Yes, very near to here," the man says.

"I live quite a bit farther along," I say. "In a completely different part of the city, really. It's not very close to here at all."

The man says, "Yes, well, we're all getting more and more spread out these days. You know how it is."

"Yes," I say.

"Well," he says.

I try not to look at him.

"Say hello to your wife for me," I say.

"Of course," the man says. "You do the same."

"Of course," I say.

"Well. Goodbye then," the man says.

I say, "Goodbye."

We shake hands. I watch him turn and walk out of the car. When the doors close, I am remembering the feel of his hand, the blueness of his eyes, and his briefcase, the unusual way he had held it under his arm.

The train begins to pull away from the station. I pick up my newspaper, open it to a place. I make a mental note to give my wife a kiss when I walk through the door, and to study her face so that I will remember it in the future.

But I know I will not remember the man on the train. I know I will not remember the way he held his cigarette, or what was wrong with his feet, or anything at all about his face. Because when I come in the door, I will kiss my wife on the cheek. I will study her face for as long as it takes. But I will not remember what an attractive man he was.

No matter what, I will not remember that. **Q**

Innocence

Papa sweet-talked, "Dolly, let's." And we went walking around our roof, even to the side where you could fall off, or get pushed off, and either way go all the way down. If you stepped onto the roof from out in the hall, you came to this side first. But first you had to get off the elevator, and walk past the stairs, and come to the fire door. Then, after you opened the fire door and stepped out, you came to the side you could die from. Anybody could die from it. But dying from it made it the better side to be on because it was where the outside wall stopped and there were bars made into a fence. If you were little like I was, you could fit your head through the bars to see the river. I saw the river on my own like that lots of times. Nobody had to hold me up. But always I held on to the bars. I was six and little. First on line in school and first in catechiz. I'm older now. Still littler than most people I stand next to. Anyway, the morning I am telling you about, I didn't have to put my head through. Papa was there. It was early. The sun wasn't sticking up big like a yellow ball yet. There was a haze. It was so hot. It must have been the hottest summer there ever was. We didn't go to the beach. We were people who never went. Why would we when there was the roof? Everything a person could ever hope to have was here. Especially on the mornings Mama was inside sleeping. Papa said it was being in our Eden. We were something, Papa and me. We were standing on the step at the doors. Not the step at the fire door, but the one at the doors Mama called the French doors but which were only doors to us. They went outside from the rooms where we lived. I remember Papa had an arm up and leaned his whole body into the door. Papa was as tall as buildings to me. It was the nicest thing to look at him and watch his chest when he breathed. Sometimes I tried to breathe with him. I think I remember him saying, "Come on, Dolly," or "We have lots to do, Dolly." Next thing I remember is we wiped our feet on the mat. The truth is, we didn't have to, except Mama was always saying to us, "Don't dirty up my rooms." But outside, the bricks were Papa's and mine. I was in my bottoms. Papa was in his trunks. My top was just my titties. How we got into our swimming things and to the doors I was too sleepy to be able to tell you. But we were standing holding on to each other. The bricks were in some places worn down and in other places, like where the drain was, sunk down. It was the summer after the summer Papa had shaved his head to get all the hair off. Or maybe it was the summer after that. Anyway, Papa had his hair back. He looked like himself in his picture.

Papa, dearest, I said.

That's what Big Ruth called him. I knew it was what Big Ruth called him. And so I called him dearest too and then just looked out at the haze. The haze looked to me like it was stuck to the city. Sometimes the buildings had needles that stuck right through the haze. It looked like something was getting hurt. The buildings made walls that stopped you from seeing Mama's billboard. Even if you were as tall as Papa, you would not be able to see it. Papa picked up the pole that we came to. Hit the pole on the bricks, beat the pole to the steps we took, put the pole in its socket. I put my hands over Papa's. I moved my hands and felt more of Papa on me. We were our wheel. We cranked the pole. Papa bent more over me. His chest touched my head. I moved my head and ear to feel him better.

Can we? I said.

Big Ruth, Papa said.

I was moving my fingers on Papa. But Papa did not pick me up, or hold me on the ledge, or let me sit on his shoulders and touch the awnings. I knew what Papa said when he said Big Ruth. But I have to tell you, I wasn't afraid of falling off Papa's shoulders. I would never fall off. Because Papa held onto my legs with his strong hands and pressed them into me. I knew I was safe on his shoulders. We went on being our wheel at all of the awnings. The sun got hotter and we got hotter. Papa's sweat was coming off on me and mine was going off on him. Our sweat kept going from him to me to him. We started going the same way without either of us saying this way or that. We passed the side where if Papa were to hold me up I could look over the ledge all the way down to the gardens in the yards. We passed our gardens on the roof. Some of the pots were down on the bricks. Up on the walls there were holders with pots with gardens in the pots. There was such green and flowers so everywhere. It made you feel you were not high up, not far from the street. It made you feel you could never die from falling. You were on safe ground. The hose was rolled on a hook on a wall across from the bars. I turned the water on and looked between the bars and saw the river. I smelled the river better here than anywhere else. But that morning there was no river smell. The haze over the river was so thick I could not see to the other side, or see up river, or down. I shook the hose straight. I turned the little wheel. I hosed Papa on his feet and legs and up his trunks. I climbed on a chair and on the table and made the water fall like rain over Papa's head. I made the hose go down and down him. I pulled out the top of his trunks, put the hose where Papa said he liked to get the water on him best. I held the hose at the top of his trunks, then moved it from the front all the way around Papa to the front.

That's my Dolly, Papa said.

What else did Mama say to Papa? Did she say, "Come back to bed?" Outside, the bricks were never clean enough for her. We were always brushing the soot off and hosing. Papa and I would say, "Look, look what we're doing." But Mama did not come to look. She liked it better being in an ice bath. Even in an ice bath Mama could go on singing and sounding prettier than all of us trying to sound like angels in catechiz. She sang her own songs with her own words mostly. Sometimes she made up words to songs I listened to on the radio. Right then she was singing so angel sweet inside. Outside, I opened my mouth and took water straight from the hose. Nothing tastes like water straight from the hose. It makes you think you're drinking from out of a lake. The way I seem to remember it, I kept the water in my mouth and let my cheeks get big. Stood up on my toes. Put my mouth on Papa's. Blew water into Papa's mouth. Listened to Papa swallow. Kissed Papa on the mouth. Held him at the back of the neck. Leaned to him. Jumped off the chair. Hooked my legs around his waist. Crossed my feet and locked him to me. He made an arm into a chair for me and walked around with me sitting on him. I hosed the gardens and the bricks and all of the roof. I hosed us. Papa kept following the way of the water to the drain. He stayed with his feet on the sides of the drain and let the water go between his feet. I took more water into my mouth again and blew into Papa's mouth again.

The best water, Papa said.

Let's play Ledge? I said.

Big Ruth, Papa said.

Let's—a little? I said.

Papa lifted me to the ledge. I was standing with Papa's hands so on the middle of me, my skin went white around the shapes his fingers made. The part of me under where his ring was hurt. I looked at the little bit of ledge in front of me and took a step. I saw my toes, my sandal, too. We were on the side of the roof that faced the brownstones and the yards and the park at the end of the street. They were so far away. But I was not afraid. I felt Papa's hands and went on taking steps. I turned out my feet. My feet just fit the ledge. It felt okay where I was. I was the Eagle. My arms were wings. Papa had me. His fingers were thick rings. We did not say anything. We did not have to say anything. I saw the trees were pink. The cars were toys to me. Mama stopped her singing. "Better not," I heard Papa say. He was not talking in his clear, strong, voice. He was talking in the voice he used to mean hurry up, or let's not let's. It was the voice I always had to figure out. He made me his wheel. I went hands down on the tops of his feet. I had him at his feet and he had me by my feet. The bricks were so hot again, I could not walk with my hands on them the way I sometimes did. What I did was kick down and make my sandals go in whispers on the bricks. I started to get the roof ready for the day. I took the cushions from where we kept them, put them in their places all around. Papa filled the charcoal in the

grill. He put the umbrellas up. By then Mama was standing at
her French doors. She was looking pretty enough to be pinned
up on a new billboard. She was wearing white things. The wind
took the skirt from between her legs. Mama had the best legs.
Right then she had the nippers in her hand and was reaching
out to a plant. She cut herself a flower and put it in her hair.
Papa was tasting Mama. I took the hose to Papa. He made his
hands into a cup for me. I held the nozzle of the hose and water
trickled until Papa's hands were full of the water. I put my
mouth on Papa's hands and drank what was in them. Wasn't
some of Papa in the water? Water from Papa's hands was better
than water from a lake. But Papa was holding his hands out for
me, and was keeping his eyes on Mama. How she cut the flower.
How she put it in her hair. How she turned. How the wind took
her skirt. How more of her legs showed. How she walked away
from him. He took a long time tasting her. When he was finished
tasting her, he looked up at the skylight, then kicked his sandal
on the grate of the drain.

They say rain, he said.

I looked up, too. I did not know why I looked up. Or what I
was looking for. I was trying to be like Papa. To stand with my
feet the way I saw he had his. To put my hands in the same places
he had his. I tried to do the things he did the way you do things
like your Papa when you're little. I can't remember if I heard the
fire door open. Someone was coming through it. It wasn't Sukie.
With Sukie I heard her holler down the bricks, "Boots, give me a
hand. Ruthie, get me a drink." I guess it was the squeak of the
hinge that had me saying to myself—well, I think I must have
been saying, "Who now? And we didn't get to play Awning."
What I saw was a block of ice come swinging out and through the
fire door. Tongs bit down into the ice. A thick fist held the handle of the tongs. The fist I was looking at did not look like the one
I was used to seeing. It was not Teddy's hand. It was not the regular iceman's hand. This fist was bigger than Teddy's. It was a
different iceman. He was big. Bigger than Papa was. If Papa was
as tall as buildings, this iceman was as big as cities. He had too

much hair on his arms, on his chest, on his face. What I saw of his face was punched in, puffed out. You know, a nose that was in too many fights and was squished. Cheeks that were puffed out and red. He must have been punched too often because he was looking meaner the more I looked at him. He made me think he would all of a sudden hit me or hit anyone if he got it in his mind to. His eyes were icier than that block of ice he was holding. He kept his hands in his pockets, thumbs hooked on his belt. His shirt was opened down the front of it. The sleeves were torn out. He was showing himself off with skin sticking out from his neck to his belt. His boots were old with cracks in their leather. They didn't have a shine on them. The bottoms of them were the thickest I had ever seen. But I could see the heels were worn down crooked. Mama, if she were on the bricks with us, would have given his boots one of her Big Ruth looks. He wasn't like Papa who cared about everything—his boots, most of all. Didn't I tell you, we called Papa, Boots? Everybody called him Boots, even me when I wasn't calling him Papa. He had more boots than an octopus has feet to put them on. Dress boots in different colors, work boots, rain boots, snow boots, boots with laces, and boots without. He kept them always shined. He even burned the old wax off to get a better shine on them. The best thing was, for the heels on his dress boots, Papa had the cobbler put on taps. I loved to listen to Papa coming down the bricks closer to me. I guess I do go on about Papa. Did I say this iceman tried standing up taller in his boots? The funny thing was, he still was not much to look at. His pants had spots on them. There was grease from, I guess, the ice truck. There were the different foods. His pants had tears in them and he moved in ways to show off more skin with hairs sticking out. I didn't want to look at him but I could not stop. He was looking at my titties. No, no, no, no, no, he wasn't looking at the skylight, or at Papa, or through the windows to see if he could see Mama. He wasn't just looking, either. He was staring. You know how you know someone is staring. You know how you can tell a thing like that. He seemed ready to eat me up and spit out my bones. He was biting down, breathing heavy breaths through closed teeth. He kicked the heel of a boot on my bricks. I walked what Mama called my sassy walk. I made it as sassy as I could get it. You know, with my feet slapping down on the bricks and my head as high as I could get it. I was being a cat. I left that iceman with just the back of me to stare at.

That all you got, just a block? Papa said.

That's all everybody gets, the iceman said.

Nobody told you about the ice baths? Papa said.

Ice baths? the iceman said.

Just drop it in the tub, iceman, and give me a hand with these, iceman, Papa said.

Hey, I fuckin bring it—that's fuckin all, the iceman said.

Watch your mouth! Forget it! Don't bother! Papa said.

I never heard Papa talk so loud or so strong. I thought Papa was going to hit the iceman. But Papa went inside, passed things through the window, left them on the windowsill. Sodas, drinks, bottles of liquor, limes and even a watermelon were lined up. The iceman finally kerplunked the ice into the tub. The tub was of a tin and the kerplunk was loud. He chopped at the ice slowly. He put the bottles in the chopped up ice slowly. He lifted the watermelon and put it in like he was putting a baby down. The whole time he did everything he went agggh and ogggh and ugggh. I think I heard him fart. The river smell never smelled like that. He kept looking over his shoulder at my titties, at all of me from my head to my toes, at me in my eyes, even.

You here, iceman? Papa said.

I can lift a watermelon, roofman? the iceman said.

Can you find more ice on your truck? Papa said.

Papa went back to whatever he was looking up at the skylight for. He lit a cigarette and talked to himself. "Better do it. She'll want me to do it." Then she walked off the step like she was stepping off her billboard. That's how the iceman looked at her, too. Like she just stepped off her billboard and here she was breathing real breaths. That iceman had a look on his face that said he couldn't believe she was real and living up on the roof. The best part was she sassed him with her walk better than I did. She had this way of walking. I always wanted to walk the way she did. But I never could. Right then she was walking for the iceman, I could tell. She was walking for Papa, too. Did she hear Papa say she? She had this way of knowing when you said something about her or said her name. She made herself be there almost on top of you before you could even hear her coming, which you never did. I never did. She sat in her chair, put her straw bag down, kicked her legs up, put her feet up on the stool, and pointed her toes. She moved the way dancers do. Mama's feet—you know the kind. You have seen the kind. She colored her nails the color of cherries. Her toes were straight, they were not bumped with bumpy things. There were times I saw Papa just looking at her feet. She had sandals on and left them tied. Papa started to untie them. He did it just right, the way he untied. She was one sandal off, one sandal on.

If I want to walk? she said.

We cooled off the bricks, Papa said.

It's so sooty out here, she said.

The bricks are clean, Papa said.

Really? she said.

He picked her up, lifted her up. He carried her to all the places he had taken me. She kicked her feet to the ends of the awnings and touched them with her toes. Papa ran with her as fast as he did when he carried me. But she did not hold him the way I did. She sat back and pushed herself back more into his arm. She let him dance with her. He was taking different steps. He did a spin with her. He spun so fast she had to hold down her skirt. Then he put her down in her chair. He lifted her feet on the stool. He untied her other sandal. He took her foot in his mouth. He put his tongue everywhere on her foot. He kept moving his tongue on her toes. She pulled her foot away from him, but not too far away. She made circles with her foot. She spread her toes out. She fanned both feet to get air on them and dry them off. That's what she wanted me to think. Papa pulled at the skirt. He pressed his hands down on her legs and on her knees. He left his hands there. She sat like she brought her fans out and they were fanning her still. It was the hottest day. It was August that had been getting our bricks hot since June. Wasn't it August? I think it had to be. I think it must have been hotter on our roof than everywhere else in the city. We were so high up. Even the haze was beginning to lift. I thought I could see the needles better. Mama wasn't looking at the needles, or the haze, or the skylight, or at how clean we got the bricks. She was looking at the iceman looking at her.

That all you brought? One puny block that's already a puddle in the tub? Don't bother to come back if all you bring is another one of those, she said.

Did he stop breathing? He stopped making funny noises and his face got red. To Mama he wasn't there. She pulled the crocheting out of her straw bag. She threaded the hook. She was crocheting squares and adding squares to squares. She was good at being with the crocheting and getting other people to feel they weren't there. I could tell she had the iceman feeling he was hose or drain or air. Maybe he was not as good as any of those. Mama stopped the hook and put a hand into her straw bag again and went on feeling for what she could not seem to find.

Ruthie, get me the mirror and lipstick. And take off those wet sandals at the French doors. Dry yourself off before you go in, she hollered.

The truth is, the mirror was my favorite thing to touch. What I liked was, it was a mirror on only one side. Papa's picture was on the other. I do not know what the word for it is, but his picture was coated shiny and was made hard. In the picture Papa had his hair and his moustache and was holding a cigarette. The mirror fit my hand just right.

Stop playing with it. Stop turning it over. Give it to me, she hollered.

What are you doing here, iceman? she hollered.

The iceman lost his tongue, I guess. She was good at making people do things like that—lose their tongues, trip over their feet. Get so mixed up they didn't know who they were. I have to say, it was fun to see her do it to the iceman. He scuffed his feet all the way down the bricks and stayed at the fire door just holding on to the knob. He did not move the knob. For the longest time he waited. Finally, he all of a sudden walked out. I let my sandals dry in quiet on the step. I went to Papa and put my hand in his. "Don't bother your father," was what I think I remember her saying before he had a chance to say his own words. She held up the mirror and kept moving it to the different places around her face. She put the lipstick on. She smoothed down an eyebrow with a finger. She pushed back some hair off her face. She went on Big Ruthing. "You mustn't make a pest of yourself. Your father has other things to do. Can't you see your father's busy." She wasn't the way she seemed to be on her billboard. Her mouth wasn't quiet with just smoke coming out of it. She made you not want to kiss her on the mouth the way you did when you looked at her billboard. Then I guess, there was the sound of boots coming closer. That iceman, he got uglier, dirtier, and smellier by the time he came back. He breathed big huffy breaths. His hair was greasy strings. He was sweating everywhere—from around his eyes, all over his face and arms and chest, off the ends of his hair, and through his falling-apart shirt. The ice was dripping down on his pants, on his boots, and on the bricks.

You call this ice? We need ice, Big Ruth hollered.

It's all that's extra on the truck, the iceman hollered.

What happened to Teddy? Where did they find you? Big Ruth hollered.

He scuffed every brick slowly. I could feel his eyes on me hurting me. Really, I knew better. Eyes can't hurt. But I think he seemed to know I was feeling the hurt. Everything he did, he did just how he wanted to do it. Take the ice, for instance. He chopped at the ice slower than before. There was a chop. A lot of time went by before there was another one. The sounds did not go the way they do if someone is really trying to do the thing fast. "Go drip in somebody else's tub," I was saying to myself. I guess what I was saying must have been there for the iceman to see on my face. Because he chopped at the ice even slower. Isn't that how it is? Just when you want somebody to hurry up, they go slower. I wasn't going to play whatever game he thought he was playing. He wasn't Papa. He was as far away from Papa as a man could get. Right down to his boots he was. What I did was step in front of Papa and start to climb. He helped me climb him. I used my feet and pushed down with my toes on his trunks. I felt Papa with my toes. I got my belly to his chest, my leg around his neck. I moved up. I was on the back of his neck. I sat on the back of his neck. I locked my feet under his arms, around his back. I pressed down on his head. I made my fingers be combs in his hair. I pushed my bottom into his shoulders, his neck. I sat on him with all of myself. With all of myself. He ran down the bricks with me. I touched all the awnings. He ran faster. With my legs I felt his heart pound hard. I listened to his breathing, then held my breath, then took a breath the same time he did. We were doing more than playing Awning. I could tell we were doing more than playing Awning. Could Big Ruth too? Papa ran me past her to all of the awnings on all of the sides of the roof. Next thing, I cannot remember if Papa said, "Be my shower," or, "Shower me," or if he gave me the nozzle of the hose to hold. Sometimes remembering for me is like the haze. One minute things are there and the next I'm not sure what is. But the next thing, the iceman was kneeling at the tub with the ice pick in his hand not even moving. I held the nozzle over our heads and sprayed the water like a shower on us. Papa was jumping and hollering for Big Ruth to come get wet with us. Then he was hollering for her not to. He let his fingers loosen up on my legs. I started to fall down him a little. He hollered that I had gotten too heavy. He could not hold me one more minute. He was going to drop me, he hollered. I fell down him more and he caught me in that way again that made the color of my skin near where he was holding me go white. There was his ring on me hurting me. The water rushed all over us. He held me up. I looked into his eyes. I liked looking into them. It was safe looking into them. They were black holes. He put me down so I was standing on the drain. He took the nozzle from me. Did he forget Big Ruth? And the iceman? Papa dropped his trunks, I dropped my bottoms. He weed into the drain. I weed into the drain. He weed on my wee. This was our Eden. I jumped into the water's rushing. I did not hear the fire door squeak. I did not hear the sound of bags crinkling. If the bottoms of shoes were coming down the bricks, I didn't hear them. She couldn't have hollered, "Ruthie, get me a drink," or "Boots, give a girl a hand." Wouldn't I have heard if she had? I guess, the way we were, Papa and I were having too much fun being Papa and me.

You two! she said.

I cannot say where the iceman was looking when Sukie came marching in. If it was at her, or at Big Ruth, or at Papa, or if he was looking at my titties. But it seems that Sukie's voice was all there was to listen to. There was no sound of the chopping. That iceman was still kneeling over the tub, acting like he was chopping when he really wasn't. Black hairs on his chest were sticking to him. He rubbed the black hairs in slow rubs with his hands always going slower. Papa had his back to him. But what that iceman didn't know was that Papa could sometimes see from somewhere inside of himself.

Finished chopping, iceman? Papa said.

The chops started to come a little faster then. I went to where we kept the towels on the cart and carried them to Papa. Papa made little pats on me with a towel and took that towel and tied it on himself. He tied a dry towel on me. I rubbed with another on his feet and all the way to where the towel he had on ended. Papa was starting to color up red. I went for the bottle of oil. I pushed a chair close to him. Its feet made such clawing sounds on the bricks that Mama peeked out from under the umbrella. She didn't bother to tie her sandals on. She ran on her toes. The wind took her skirt again. She put her face close to Papa's. She did not have to stand on her toes to put her mouth on his. She was sweet-talk and kisses. "Daddy honey, I'll put it on for you," she said. She took the bottle of oil out of my hand. Poured some. Put her hand near Papa's nose and kept it there. He smelled and smelled the oil. She put her feet inside his feet. Her skirt went on his legs and between them. She stroked him with the oil with slow strokes. He moved his mouth on all of her face. She oiled all of his face. She put a hand on his chest and stayed so on him there was little room for her hand to fit. Then she turned him. Oiled his back. Kneeled. Oiled the backs of his legs. She put more oil on him with her fingers going around his legs where she knew the tops of his boots would be. She hosed off her hands and rubbed them dry on the towel he had on. She brought him his boots, his socks, his dry trunks. She kneeled again. She held the trunks for him to step into. She went up his legs with them to where if he had on pants he would have on a belt. She untied the towel he had on and let it fall. She put the socks in his hand and pushed them down into the middle of his hand. In her most cottony Big Ruth voice she called out.

Your ice is melting, iceman.

I went to the leaves near the bars and made-believe no one was here on my bricks—no Mama, no iceman, no Sukie. From where I was I could see through the bars though I was not sticking my head between them. Papa and I were going up river. Papa was saying, "Dolly, this river smells sweet." It smelled sweeter the more I smelled it. It is nice to river dream. Salena was the one who taught me how. She used to take me to the river sometimes after catechiz, sometimes to let Mama get a good soak in an ice bath, sometimes any old time. We sat down on a patch of grass and did our looking. Salena started river dreaming out loud. She always started the same way. "Once upon a time, I had me a red petticoat. I had me a man to wear it for. He were fine. He had on patent leather shoes, a silk vest, and a stick pin with a stone in it big as a star. He took me up river on a riverboat. He gave me times to dream about." It was always the same beginning with Salena and after that every river dream was different. It was long since Salena went down home the way she did every summer. It would feel longer still until she came back, and I sank my face into her big titties, and heard her say, "Child, let's us go river dream." I was the one who decided if Salena could river dream with me on a patch of grass, I could river dream for myself from the roof. That's what I did without telling anyone. I didn't tell

Papa, even. Except now that I'm telling you—nobody knows about my river dreaming. I guess I am happiest river dreaming. But Sukie wouldn't let me be happy being in the leaves wearing just the towel I had on. I heard her say, "Where is she? What's she doing? Why isn't she here?" She talked a long list while she was going through the bags making crumpling sounds with all of the tissue. She pulled out a dress and veil. She called out my name. I leaned down into the leaves. From where I was I could see the iceman.

You let her go around like that? Sukie said.

Like what? Big Ruth said.

Isn't it time for her to wear more? Sukie said.

She's a child, Big Ruth said.

Everybody looks, Sukie said.

Who looks? Big Ruth said

It was so hot. I could have stayed in the leaves and river-dreamed to a place too far from Sukie to ever hear her. Nothing was perfect enough for Sukie. She always had to change things. Do this. Do that. Don't. She was the one who made Big Ruth send me to catechiz. She was the one who said a child needs to get religion and that Big Ruth and Boots were heathens. Big Ruth said it was easier to say okay to some of the things Sukie said because Sukie had the power to box the ears off an angel and there was no way Big Ruth could get to be one of those. That was Sukie. I remember her ironing things with her hands. Pulling at collars and doing what even Big Ruth said was too much primping. I leaned into the leaves more. What I think I remember next was the haze started making so much noise. Still over the sounds of it I heard Carlos say, "Preciosa there you are." I guess the wind took some of the leaves off me. "I see you in the leaves, Preciosa," I think I heard Carlos say. It was impossible for me to make-believe I didn't hear him say, "Preciosa, come hold the door for me." He didn't pick up the loose brick that was there and use it. I guess he just wanted me to do it. To tell you the truth, I thought helping Carlos would be better than trying on the dress and veil for Sukie. What I did was walk past

Papa. He lit a cigarette and sucked and puffed and talked to himself. He was saying that whoever did the putting on, put the wrong nails in. That's what made them fall out and come down on the bricks. It was the wrong nails in the flashing. Because he wasn't seeing me, I didn't think, I didn't stop. I walked by him. I had to walk by the iceman, too. It was then I decided this is who the iceman was. He was the Devil. The Devil, just like I saw him in the pictures I looked at in catechiz. Everything about him was the Devil. He had the same face, the same everything. The only different thing was the Devil had a pitchfork and the iceman had an icepick. When he wasn't chopping with it, he put it through a loop on his belt. It was always right there, easy for him to pick up and use. I held the fire door with my whole body leaning to it. I was keeping that big, heavy fire door back against the wall good. First, Carlos was carrying the metal strips for the flashing and a can of nails. He kept coming past me and going back out and doing it again. Next, the ladder he was carrying hit into the door frame. Next, he was carrying aprons. Next, Sukie was in front of me breathing on me, shaking the dress and veil.

Now, she said.

Do I gots to? I said.

She's talking pickaninny again. You should get rid of that Salena, she said.

Bring me somebody who cleans as clean, Big Ruth said.

Salena would have said, "What you riling Miz Sukie for? You knows better." I did know better. But I don't know, without Salena every summer got too hot for too long. Riling Sukie felt as good to me as a cold drink of water. I knew now was now to Sukie. I knew Carlos had less than a second to pick up the loose brick and put it in place. That didn't stop me from giving Sukie a kiss on the mouth long and hard enough to pick up the color she had on her mouth. I like to get a little color on my mouth sometimes. But Sukie was quick to pull me off the bricks and inside with a tug. I have to tell you, Mama's fans felt good to me. I spread my arms and was the Eagle and the fans felt even better. Sukie untied the knot in the towel I had on and put the dress on me. I stopped feeling nice and started feeling hotter. The dress had little tiny buttons puffed like pincushions were inside of them with eyelets made of thread to catch the buttons on. The lace was webs with the shapes of flowers in them. Was I supposed to care? What Papa was saying to Carlos outside was what I cared about. He was saying something about putting new shingles on. He said how if he put them on in a special way, that would keep the water out. There was a way to do things right, he said. Sukie's fingers went fast up my back buttoning me into the dress. I do not know how long it was I held my breath. But I had to hold it. Sukie finally unbuttoned the dress and let me breathe. Still she made me keep the dress on. The whole time we were inside Sukie tried to make an angel out of me even though it was too hot to try to be one. She kept saying what an angel I was, what an angel I looked like. The truth is, Sukie was making me more into a pincushion, I thought. She put pins between her teeth, took them out one and then another, and stuck them where the buttons should go. She was good at holding the pins between her teeth and talking at the same time. Somehow she got it into her head that she had to have me practice the catechiz. Getting the buttons right went like this. "How many persons are there in God?" Stick. "There are three divine persons in God." Stick, stick. "Who are they?" Stick, stick, stick. "They are the Father, the Son, and the Holy Ghost." Stick, stick, stick, stick. What Sukie did not know was that Salena would never let me go without knowing the catechiz. There were days when I asked Salena to river dream but she said, "This ain't no time for river dreaming. We gots to learn you that catechiz so you be wearing that dress and veil on that day you is supposed to." The funny thing was, the more I got the answers right, the more Sukie made me into a pincushion. I breathed. She put the veil on my head and spread her fingers under it and made it puff out. I think it must have been okay. Sukie didn't try to make it more perfect. But she needed to work on me. "Remember, you will be the first on line," she said. "Put your hands together. Point your fingers up to God. Stand up straight. Take slow steps. Everyone will be looking," she said. I felt like the sun was coloring me up through stained glass. I went to the step by the French doors and stood there.

Big Ruth, what to you think? she said.

Better get her out of it before she dirties it, Big Ruth said.

Did Big Ruth even look? That iceman looked. All Big Ruth did was put a hand down into her straw bag again. Inside the straw bag Big Ruth kept lots of things. I watched her go with her hand all the way to the bottom where the straw sits on the bricks and you can feel the hard of the bricks and the hot of the bricks coming through. I have been there. I could not see exactly what Big Ruth took out and had tucked in her hand. But I knew what she had to have from seeing her go into her straw bag so many times before. She put the mirror near her mouth and with the lipstick started fixing. Talk about primping—Sukie was hardly a primper compared to Big Ruth when she was fixing her mouth. Papa used to say the world would take her mouth home with them, if they could. She had that kind of a mouth. She turned the mirror over and took a look at Papa. It seemed she liked to look at him, then at herself. It seemed she liked to hold the mirror. It did have the best way of fitting in your hand and feeling good to you. I've never seen another mirror like it. She had it made before he went off to war. That thing she had done to his picture— that whatever it was that made it shiny and hard—she had done before the war. He still looked the same. He didn't look any older. Right then he was busy talking to Carlos. The way he was talking all of him was doing it. The longer he talked, the blacker I saw his eyes get. Carlos kept going no, no, no, with his head. Carlos had to feel Papa's eyes were talking louder to him than the haze. But Papa's eyes were not the iceman's eyes. That iceman— his eyes made me feel that he was going to pick me up and throw me off the roof. With Papa it was different. He was talking to Carlos in a way, I thought, that seemed just Papa and Carlos were there on the roof for each other. After a bit Carlos went yes, yes, yes, and went out.

Mexican runt, Papa said.

You got what you wanted? Mama said.

I got. He's bringing his Rosa and their kid up here for the day, Papa said.

Not that thing she wears in a sack? Mama said.

I don't know, Papa said.

Don't expect me to do anything for them, Mama said.

The truth is, I could not wait to get out of that dress. I was squirming when Sukie unpinned me. At least, that's what I remember her saying—stop it, stop that squirming. I put on my shorts and ran out to the bricks. I picked up my sandals, put them on, buckled them. The iceman was kneeling at the tub, playing with the ice he wasn't chopping, playing with the sodas and the watermelon. He kept moving things around and sinking them down into the water. He kept looking at Big Ruth, then at me. Big Ruth made her mouth go even better than it did on her billboard. First she made-believe she was going to blow smoke. Then she puckered her mouth and stared at that iceman. She huffed slow huffs so deep I could hear them where I was. She licked her mouth wet. Anybody would want to put his mouth on hers right then. That iceman—he was making Devil eyes and a Devil mouth. But Big Ruth didn't let him bother her. She was used to people doing funny things.

Chop me some ice this big, Big Ruth said.

She held up her hand, her fingers just so wide apart for the iceman to see. So then he chopped to how big she wanted. So then he gave her this piece of ice all dripping on itself and on him. She took it. Put it to her tongue. Licked it. Then she put it up her skirt. She spread her legs more than they already were. She put the ice up higher. Her skirt bunched up around her. I could not see all the way to where she went with the ice. But when her hand came out from under the skirt without the ice, I knew where she had left it. I knew Big Ruth. I knew Papa too. He made-believe he was busy putting up the ladder, getting it closer to the skylight. But he was seeing with the back of his head the way that he did. That iceman took to Mama's Big Ruthing like it was sweet-talk. He let a smile go across his face so big he had me almost thinking someone gave him a present.

Ain't you that dame on the billboard? Yeah, you're that dame on the billboard, he said.

Mama just breathed a slow breath. She picked up the hook and started to crochet. Sukie hollered out, "Somebody fix me a drink." I made-believe I didn't hear her. I walked the bricks to Papa. The back of Papa's neck was getting red. Mama did not oil him good. I picked up the bottle of oil and stood at his boot waiting. I made it clear to him in the way I always did that I was ready to climb. He gave me a lift up. I gave him the cap I took off and the bottle to hold. He poured the oil into my hands. I put my hands around him there on the back of his neck. I kept the oil going around with my hands on his neck then on his face. I took my sweet time. Still, too soon he put me down. The bricks felt hard to me after the feel of him. He said, "Better get those drinks." And I went past Mama on my way to the tub. She stopped moving the hook and looked into me somewhere so deep I felt her eyes inside of me there.

Cuntlet, she said. **Q**

ELEANOR ALPER

Today : Cookeys
Tomorrow : The Wurld

TO SHIRLEE T. OV HOLLYWOOD:

Frum Stella. Ov Upper Blak Eddy. Up wair. Weer groe win Speshull ROOTS heer. Witcht ROOTS. Alongd width Speshull Weeds heer. Asd well as Speshull Stems. & Buds. & Bulbs. & Barks. & Wyilld Seeds. Like for rinstints Snayk Root. & Boen Set. & Lung Wort. Is wot Iyim yewsin in MYE COOKEYS. Witcht COOKEYS Shirlee. Wots beein mayd asd I sed. Frum thees Speshull. & long forgottin. & old fashunnd ROOTS & the Sutch. Are taystin so GOOD Thair Sellin heer like Hot Cayks. & tallkin ov wots old. Thoe not forgottin. & wye Iyim Riten to yew Shirlee? Inasted ov Riten. Say. To Liz T. Hoos allsto gettin old. Not that Lizziz lookin it. Butt frum Lizziz laytlee goe win on so menny Dyits. & taykin it ALL offt. & goe win orffa thoes Dyits. & puttin it ALL bak on. Is wye. Deependin on wethur Lizziz orffem. Or onnem. Is how cum Liz mite not wanna tayst a CRUM. Ov wun ov MYE COOKEYS. Like yewll bee wantin to Yor sellft. Seeins how yewv stayd so Thin. & so Trim. & Shirlee. Eevind so Yung. Cunsidderrin ov Yor Ayj & all. Is wye. Aftur yew tayst MYE Sampill COOKEY. Downd innside Mye Paddid Mayill Bagg. Wot Bagg Shirlee. Is sittin on Yor lap now. Unlesst yewd allredeed ET it. Frum MYE COOKEYs lookin GOOD enuf to EET. Is how I noe wot yewll bee sayin? . . . Or yewd allreddy sed. Is dont Stellas COOKEY tayst GRAYT? & Betterin enny COOKEY I evvur yet ET Thoe Shirlee. Maybee yewd say AYT. Butt ennyways Shirlee. Dont yew want MOR? & dont yew wanna Bank Role me. Not that Iyidbee needin a Hole Role. Beeins owenly Haaf a Role mite do. So Shirlee how abowt ME & YEW. Beecummin COOKEY Bizzniss Partnurs. Bye goe win Fiftee Fiftee. Or Fortee Fortee. Sinnst width MYE COOKEYS. & Shirlee. Yor MUNNY. Beesides ov Yor Faymuss Naym. & eevin wun ov thoes old Baybee Pitchurs ov yew. Eetin a COOKEY. All the wyillst Yor lookin so Smylee & so Kewt.

Asd yew allways yewsta. Dimplin up Yor littil Dimpull. Bak then. Wen yew lookt GOOD enuf to eet Yor sellft. Is wot Pitchur we cood put on Top ov eetcht & evvry Boxx ov MYE COOKEYS. Witcht Naym Shirlee. Iyid bee glad to chaynj to ARE COOKEYS. Or eevin to Stellas & Shirlees COOKEYS. Or bettur still. To Shirlees & Stellas COOKEYS. Or iffin Yor INSISSTIN. Iyid go so FAR. Asd callen em SHIRLEES COOKEYS. Asd long as its sayin sumwairs BIG on that Boxx. Thees RESSAPEES are BYE STELLA ov Upper Blak Eddy. & aftur weev sold Thowzins. & maybee Millyins. Ov ARE COOKEYS. & weer maykin BIG BUKS. & rolen in DOE. Meenin in MUNNY. Is wen Iyim gornna MOOV Mye sellft to Hollywood. To Yor Fifth Air Vinyew thair. Or Yor Park Playce thair. Or leestin to Yor Marvins Gardins. & go shoppin Acrosst the Oshins. In that Cuntree ov PARRIS. Saym asd wair Yor shoppin Shirlee. For PARRIS Purrfewms. Like Eevnin In PARRIS. & wot evvur thair maykin. Frum that Plasstur ov PARRIS. & abowt MUNNY? Wuzzint it sed in wun ov thoes SAYINS. Witcht SAYINS mite ov bin sed. Asd far bak. Asd bak in the Bible. Frum beein so TRU. Is how yew cann NEVVUR bee tew RITCHT. Or tew FAYMUSS. So Shirlee. Woodint yew like to bee asd RITCHT & asd FAYMUSS as yew wunst WUZ? Bak wen yew wur maykin Yor Shirlee Moovees. & Yor Shirlee Dolls then. & Shirlee Books then. & Shirlee Paypur Dolls. Wen we still had Paypur Dolls. & maykin Mayk beeleev Shirlee Kiddee Stoevs. Wots all havvin Yor Pitchur on em. & Yor Naym on em. So Hoo wuz gettin all that MUNNY frum Sellin em? Wuz YEW Shirlee. & how I noe abowt Yor Shirlee Stuff Shirlee? Is findin Yor Stuff at the Dump. Witcht Dump they wur callin the Lannd Filld. Witcht thair now callin the Ree Sykilin Sentur. Thoe its Filld still width Garbij. Butt Shirlee I say. Wunst a Dump allways a Dump. Well ennyhows. How I fownd Yor Shirlee Stuff. Is wyill Poek kin arownd in that Garbij thair. Seeins Iyim seein it like yesturday. Width me on Mye Hannds & Mye Nees. Witcht is how yew had to Poek. For moestly for Bottils. For taykin to the Stor. For MUNNY. Sinnst weer POOR heer. & iffin yew cann beeleev it Shirlee? Bak THEN. We wuz eevin POORUR. So thair. In that saym Garbij. In that saym Dump. Is wair Iyim spottin this Car Ruggaytid Boxx.

Wots Stufft to the Gills width Yor Shirlee Stuff. & dumpt maybee bye sum FAN ov Yors. Not likelee livvin thoe in Upper Blak Eddy. Wair asd I sed. We wuz POOR. Butt livvin sum playce RITCHT. Like in Tinacum or Erwinna. Wair thayd ov had the MUNNY for byin Yor Iggspensiv Shirlee Stuff. Sinnst Tinacum & Erwinna are still dumppin thair Iggspensiv Garbij up bye us. Witcht is wye Iyim still lookin in that Dump. & findin this Typin Riten Misheen. Is how Iyim Riten. Butt Shirlee. Bak to that FAN ov Yors. Hoo maybeed bye thenid. Bin all groed up. Or wuz eevin DED Like Kids wuz droppin DED like Flys then. Frum the Feevurs. Speshully RITCHT Kids. Witcht Kids wuzzint eetin enny ROOTS like we wuz. Or Shirlee. Maybee that FAN ov Yors. Jusst got FED up width yew. Beeins wen I fownd Yor Boxx ov Shirlee Stuff. Wot Iyim SAD to say. Is Shirlee. Yew wur allreddy a HAD BIN. Butt Hoo wuz BIG then? & wuz Riden HYE then? & for a good long wyill aftur that then Shirlee. Wuz Jewdee G. Frum goe win Ovur the Rayn Boe. Thoe bye nows. Its all Worter Undur the Brij. & abówt Brijjiz Shirlee. Wair Iyim sellin Mye COOKEYS? Is bye side the Brij. At Maddim Yewlannas Beeyewtee Boxx. Witcht is wair I got Yor Hollywood Addresst. Beeins Maddim Yewlanna is all-sto frum Hollywood. So Shirlee. Izzint it a smorll Wurld? Butt bak to MYE COOKEY Wyillst Yor still now taystin it. Or leestin. Taystin the aftur tayst. & Shirlee. Dont it still tayst Grayt? & wot ellst beesides ov ARE COOKEYS we cood sell? Is thoes Speshull ROOTS. & the Seeds. & the Sutcht. To wuns wantin to bayk THAIR COOKEYS. Thair Sellfts. Is wye thayill bee needin ARE COOKEY COOKBOOK & Hooill bee havvin to Rite it? Is nun uthur butt ME & YEW. Width ME tellin YEW wot to Rite. & YEW doin the Riten. Sinnst Shirlee. ME. Iyim not so GOOD ov a Riter. & wye Iyim yewsin this Riten Misheen? Is frum not goe win mutcht to Skool. Not that we dinnint hav Skools. Butt yew needid Shooz to go to Skool. So I wuz moestly at the Dump. Inasted ov at the Skool. Poek kin threw that Garbij for Shooz. Asd well as for Bottils. Is wye Iyim the Luckey Kid findin Yor Shirlee Stuff. Wyillst the uthur Kids. Havvin Shooz. Are in Skool lernnin to Rite. Witcht reeminds me ov wot ellst we mite do. Aftur ARE BOOK got all

Rote? & weer dun cowntin ARE MUNNY & weev livvd Hye enuf on thoes Hollywood Hogs. In beetweend ov byin owt thoes PARRIS Shops. & bye then. Wair BOTHT gettin kindov BORRD. Is wen we mite mayk Yor Shirlee Dolls aggen. Thoe inasted ov that Doll beein a Moovee Star. This new Doll cood bee a COOKEY Baykur. Wots wairrin a Cooks Aprin. & a Baykurs Hat. & beeins that Hattill bee flattnin owt Her pritty Shirlee Curls. Wot Yewlanna sed? Is wye not mayk sum Shirlee Doll Curliz. Width Yor Pitchur on em. Ov corst. & iffin thay go ovur BIG & Shirlee wye shoodint thay? Then nexxt. We cood mayk Shirlee Doll Home Permamint Wayv Kits. & then aftur all that Curlin & Permmin. Wen that Shirlee Dolls Hair gets so fullov Split Tid Ennds. Like Enndsill get. & that Hairs startin to fall owt. Wot abowt maykin Shirlee Doll Wigs? Is allsto wot Yewlanna is sayin. Witcht is wye Yewlanna is wantin a CUT OV ARE Bizzniss. For leestin for the Hair Part. & Shirlee wye not? Sinnst dinnint Yewlanna. Frum beein frum Hollywood. Giv me Yor Hollywood Addresst? & to tell the trewth. Sinnst I Pride Mye sellft on beein Onnist. & seeins weer gornna bee Bizzniss Partnurs & all. Hoo DREEMT up this Hole COOKEY Bizzniss Ideer ennyways? Is Yewlanna. Frum havvin asd she has. A GOOD Bizzniss Hed. Frum havvin a Bizzniss her sellft. Meenin her Beeyewtee Boxx. Wair Iyim sellin MYE COOKEYS. & Hoo TEW? Is thoes Ritcht & Fanssee Laydees frum Tinacum & Erwinna. The wuns Yewlanna is callin The Gurls. Witcht Gurls are cummin to the Beeyewtee Boxx. Aftur dumppin thair Garbij at the Dump. For gettin Cut & Curld. & maybee Permd. & eevin Bleetcht Owt. & Frorstid Ovur. & Dyid. Not to menshun sum. Iffin yew cann beeleev it? Cummin in for gettin thair Curls mayd Strayt. Wyill all the wyill eetin MYE COOKEYS. Witcht COOKEYS thair bringgin Home in Baggs. To eet in Tinacum & Erwinna. So Shirlee we cood bring ARE COOKEYS to playssiz Farrin. Like to PARRIS wen weer shoppin thair. Or sennd em eevin Farrur. Like ovur to Affrika. Wair yewv bin wurkkin for thoes Yewnytid Nayshuns. Is wot Yewlanna sed. & Hoo noes Shirlee? Width all Yor Farrin & Yewnytid Cunnekshuns. & Mye Speshull ROOTS. Iffin sumday. ARE COOKEYS mite not get to go OVUR the Rayn

Boe. In wun ov thoes Owtur Spayst Ships. & bee shippt Kleer up to the MOON.

    Frum Stella
    Waytin
    To Heer
    & This PS Is For Sayin.

Wair thoes Speshull ROOTS are groe win Shirlee? Is allsto up bye that Dump. Asd yew mite ov gesst. Beein it wuz thair. Wair I fownd Yor Boxx ov Shirlee Stuff. So Shirlee. Not that Iyim puttin enny Wurds in Yor Mowth. Thoe wot yew cood say? Witcht Iyim sayin heer Mye sellft. Is. ARE COOKEY Bizzniss. Musstov bin mayd in Hevvin.

    Frum Stella
    Still
    Waytin
    & This PS.

Abowt Yor Mayk Beeleev Shirlee Kiddee Stoevs. Is for Mye sayin. Not that Iyim cumplaynin. Butt Shirlee. That Shirlee Stoev. Wot wuz lookin still like new then. Nevvur got Warm enuf. To Warm a COOKEY. Nevvur mind Hot enuf. To Bayk a COOKEY. & thoe that Stoev wuz owenly Asspoesd to bee Mayk Beeleev. Yew allways wantid it to bee Reel. Or leestin me. So Shirlee. Iffin we DO dee side. To mayk thoes Shirlee Stoevs aggen. & wye Not? Sinnst ARE Shirlee Doll is gornna bee a COOKEY Baykur. Coodint ARE new Shirlee Stoevs. Bee REEL Littil Kiddee Minnee Mykro Wayvs

    Frum Stella
    Cowntin The Days
    Till Yew Rite
    & Shirlee This PS Is For Sayin.

In the cayst Yor wundrin wye Maddim Yewlanna lefft Hollywood? & is livvin in Upper Blak Eddy? Is frum her beein so Paytree Yotik. She maireed a Soljur. & got to bee a War Bride. Like Yewlanna sed yewd allsto got. & Shirlee. Wot ellst Yewlanna sed? Is how Shirlee T had enuf Sennts thoe. To leev that NO GOOD Soljur ov hers. & go bak to Hollywood. Butt Shirlee. Wot yew allsto musstov had. Beeins yew wuz still so RITCHT then. Wuz the Dolliz. To go width the Sennts.

Frum
Yor FAN
Stella
& Shirlee This Lasst PS Is For Sayin.

Iffin it haddint ov bin for that War then. Wood Yewlanna ov evvur gottin up. To Upper Blak Eddy? So wair wood I bee Sellin MYE COOKEYS? & Hoo ellst butt Yewlanna. Woodov DREEMD up ARE COOKEY Bizzniss? & woodov had Yor Hollywood Addresst? Is wye Iyim thankkin GOD for that War Shirlee. & shoodint yew bee tew?

Frum Stella
Hoos Allsto
Thankkin GOD
For YEW **Q**

They were oblivious to my
gaze

The Ascension

Miss Kelly raises
the wild child up
to the jungle
bars, her rose
blouse lifting

the worth of one rung,
so that I notice,
in the navel,
what looks
like a discolored pearl,
or like a purple clot of flesh.

Tarnished

Oh, what in us
is there else?
We do not go well.
Most live seldom.
So few sing.

Can we not know
the cicada leaves
a shellskin?
A little tuba
left to glisten
below the golden elm.

Fun House

A number of house plants
go through
what is called a
rest period,
when growth appears to stop and,
in some cases,
all they want to do
is eat pussy.

Greek Line-up

Parmenides rf
Zeno 2b
Anaxagoros 1b
Democritus cf
Melissus 3b
Empedocles 1f
Heraclitus c
Pythagoras ss
Thales p

Flaubert's Kitchen

People are like food.
Most people are like Cool Whip.
Whoever's left over
are like Slim Jims,
Spam,
Wonder Bread,
or Jell-O.
Maybe even Tater Tots.

Business District

Advice.
Lemonade.
Toy Hats.
Closed.

Apollinaire in America

This bus courses over the bones of America.
The wisdom of each prairie
rolled up into tumbleweed
about to blow away.

One riverbed is flooded with light;
you weep without knowing why.
Somewhere north of there,
in the great cathedral of dust,
horses gallop.

The Right Fielder

Drawing close to the billboard, he loses the ball to the
    lights.
He lifts his mitt, guessing at the ball that pours across
    leather and streams
through the hands of a disbelieving fan. The dust
    does not give up his shame,
nor his wife's suffering in the seats. Walking
    back to the dugout,
he listens to voices that chastise.
"Rodriguez," the short manager breathes, the one
who would always be knuckling in his life now,
who got him the job working for Dow.
His name is a withered flower.
He hears the fans lose their voices again
    in the ninth, sees the clear water
of the moon out early in its judgment.
He turns, his few remaining pesos to melt into
    the neighborhood.
He stares into the manager's face that knows
    where he is going and what
he will be doing, what he will look like in the morning,
    and asks himself if ever
there will be a day without this knowledge.

After the Game

He kicks at the dirt, raising cigarette butts and candy
wrappers at home plate. They drove all night from
Oaxaca to lose to the Mexico City Kings, and he
sees the long way back to that crowd in Oaxaca,
will find the grave already dug for his mitt. So he
dreams of his body exploding against the billboard,
the ball dropping before him on the grass, the
runners moving around the basepaths, their legs
striving for the wheat-colored plate. He lifts up an
arm, as if at the last minute he could catch something other than the state of a janitor with a broom.

The Caller

Always calls
in the morning or
late at night

he must have
a busy life

there is never a sound
in the background—
not even breath

something considerate
about him

without a voice
he loves me.

A Man I Knew

has a condo

a maid who comes
every other week

kids who won't

are on the dresser
they float forever

like a boat

In Tina's House

I am slicing the dog's legs off
while talking.
I don't even remember the conversation.
The dog never complained.
Good dog.
Later, we'll go for a walk.

After Getting Rid of Ben

I slept well.
Deeply and peacefully.
I woke up
light as a bird—
    there were feathers
    all over everything.

Events Leading Up to It

All day long
she hears a low growling
behind her. She decides
they aren't there.
Maybe they'll go away. Instead,
they begin following closer.
She can feel their warm breath, though
no one on the street acknowledges it.
She realizes she is alone; turns,
fires at them.

According to Aunt Rose

Her generation
never ate beans or
told the truth recklessly
or drove with nothing
on its mind.

The Way Father Ate an Apple

Was to cut it and remove
the pocket of seeds
from each half.
Next, he peels away the skin
in strips, and cuts
each half of the fruit
into quarters, then each
quarter in half.
One each day.
Either a Rome or a Winesap.

Brink-Grasses

He saw a man led bound with both his arms
behind his back along a mountain path.
Two soldiers with Winchesters ushered him
down to the village where the circuit judge
awaited him for sentencing. His crime was grave.
Great-uncle Albert wrote, "I've seen a man
force-marched toward his death. He didn't flinch
nor did he stumble. I say, he *strode*
(that fine old verb conveys his dignity)
down the jagged pebbles of the mountain road.
And yet, almost immediately, I found myself
imagining the heart at work in his chest,
the little, laboring handful of his heart,
and everything I saw thereafter on the path
entered memory indelibly,
as though I saw them with that bound man's eyes.
My own heart ghosted me all down the slope."

He hung on the scraggled shocks of grass
that held with hysterical flourishes to the brink
of the gorge and prospered dustily above the abyss.
Too literary, Albert, that, too apposite.
Rather, let your newfound eyes assimilate
the drab speckles on the pebbles' backs
spotted like old men's hands and how the foul
insinuating dust your passing kicked
clotted your nostrils, nested in your eyelashes
and tasted like chimney soot along your tongue.
"Maybe he was acquitted, after all. Maybe
the judge, grown drowsy in a cloud of flies,
indulged discretion and gave clemency . . . ."

For decades Albert heard the rifle shots
when half-asleep, or felt the scratchy rope—
he who espoused the "manliness of Christ"
spurned fear as womanly, unmanly, weak—
and dreamed a rippling dream of brink-
clinging grasses over abysmal paths
and dreamed of hanging like a clutch of grass
at the lip of the cliff, and only there,
torn between sleep and falling, did
this distant Albert feel himself alive.

Great-Uncle Albert Renounces
the Apocalypse

Dear Sisters,

My suit is white with dark mixed in, a dark
coat, rather long, a
cutaway style that's all
the go up here. Don't think
I'm getting swell! A young fellow
must look his best to get ahead. Last
evening, after the dance, in my new clothes I drove
my horse and sleigh back home along Lake George.
(My horse is cloud-colored and loves the frost.)
After an hour, both my hands were freezing
to the reins. Sisters, it was beautiful.
The mud had turned to something diamond
the runners hopped and skidded upon and my breath
was so spiky that it clittered in the mountain air.
For miles and miles the lake
looked nickled over. Instead of
aspirating possibilities, instead
of proffering my ambitious fingers to the breeze,
instead of pleasuring in the pure and lonely air
a fright came over me as though I stood
before some smelter or some smoky vat
where something terrible was being alloyed.

You know I have an allergy to prophets.
When Papa would declaim from *Lamentations*, my
only shivers were for the homespun city of
    Jerusalem,
and I pictured it as homespun out of old, worn
    stone.

Sisters, on that icy night
a memory of Maman's washing hung out to dry
came to my mind and made me
whoop against the cold.
All the clothes her hands had rubbed and
scoured and wrung!
I thought of the way women love to fold fresh clothes.

Dear Sisters, after that uncompanionable
drive from Lake George homeward
with my frost-nibbling horse
atrot, I reckon I will abjure
Judgment Day and every end of days and every cold
intransigence of purpose no matter how
obdurate the ice it nests among.
I hold the promises of Jerusalem against Judgment Day.
It will be lovely as a Tuesday line of wash.

Your Loving Brother,
A. Milmow
Schenectady, 1894

RALPH ADAMO

Roches Moutonnées

Whoever let language into the house goes
men talking about their jumpy keys
the dream that outsilences them as they walk along
the little night following the little day
only the extravagant stranger carries a pepper pouch
    in hunting season
someone has the books to prove it
the line light to true it the hello
the musical lie down and trickle grin simplification
horses on the air
a tatter on the horizon the juice torn out of it
the onion hanging in the beef

A Voice That Won't Sing

It was my fault.
She could have gone either way.
She sat up in bed,
awash in flannel, considering
the mechanics of the move.
The unhad dream clutched in the plains
of her heart. The beam
rolled from the fire that took its time
and fell. The markets shut down.
Desire, death, all of them,
attending the wake of affluence
cornered in its bright cantina.
It was my fault.
The song mumbled in the river.
Away, away still
farther, like a token of human life
tracked away from the star
seeking the star.

1976: A Closure

You get back in the car, this time
move closer to the door, take your hands
out of his lap, put the cap back on
the gin, pull your pantyhose back up,
fasten all the hooks, the hooks.

Latin Quarter

The hotel had two stars, a single
Elevator, a bathroom down the hall,
One bed in the room I took.

The first thirty seconds outlasted
My first twenty-one years, and then
Our limbs touched.

While it was still dark, we dressed,
Jumped the turnstile in the subway,
And went to Sacre Couer.

When dawn came, the gods began
To speak. The same morning
I returned to England.

Lord Nelson

Applied Bonaparte's
Rule of concentration

To warfare at sea.
Dying at Trafalgar,

He sent his love to Lord
Collingwood and, like

An innocent schoolboy,
Retiring to bed, said,

"Kiss me, Hardy,"
And turned to die.

Carlyle

He walked through the British Museum
In silence, believing a sincere man
Will see something and say nothing.

Lighting his cigar at Stonehenge,
He told Emerson the American has two
Choices—stay in London, be a man

And confront the English, main force
To main force, or run away to France,
Where one cannot speak without lying.

Wordsworth

In his very narrow
And English mind

He carried a hundred
Lines. Never hurried

To publish, never
Praised anybody.

Wrote poems without
The aid of war.

Wrote longer than
He was inspired.

Sidney Lanier

He played the flute his father gave him
Through his youth and then the War,

Hiding it in his sleeve at the gates
Of Point Look-Out Prison. At War's end,

Consumption took his mother. Three years
Later, Lanier coughed up blood, writing:

"I do not understand this." He quit
Law with his father, moved to Baltimore,

And gave himself to music and poetry.
Wholly unacquainted with literary people,

He began to master English verse—
Whitman he considered, "poetry's butcher,"

And thought Poe did not know enough.
His course in Shakespeare lost money.

At thirty-five, he issued his poems
Written between hemorrhages, breathing

Pine and clover blossoms to delay
The final illness, before which he wrote

"The Marshes of Glyn," knowing somewhere
The heart that needs it will find it.

George Washington

Writing his nephew Lund, who gave
Supplies to a British gunboat,
For the protection of Mount Vernon:

"It would have been a less painful
Circumstance to me to have heard that
In consequence of your non-compliance

With their request, they had burnt my
House and laid the Plantation in ruins."
A man steeped in his own temperament.

CHARLES STEWART ROBERTS

Note to Grandmother Roberts

Mrs. Roberts please mam
Help me to fine something to do
or please lend me five Dollars
until the 4th of February
I will certainly pay you back
I want to get me some Coal and food
or I will come out and wash your clothes
and Clean your house and please
let me know if you can do it
for me, Your humble servant
    Mattie Wilson
PS if your boys got any children
I will Wash for them
Scrub Do anything please
for Lord sake help me

The Encyclopedia Says

To spin, the spider must press her
spinnerets against some object to
force the liquid silk out of glands,
then move off quickly, draw the sticky
substance out, which hardens in the air.
What do I best do next? she says, keep
my spinnerets together to make one thick
thread, or hold them apart for a band of
finer strands? You'll need a flashlight
to watch. She won't begin till nightfall.

On Spears

First, there was Achilles, spearing
Hector through the neck with a "pole
heavy with bronze." Early Persians
added a spike to the other end so both
could be employed. Then Romans shortened
matters—the *pilum* was born, without
which history wouldn't be the same.

The Gauls, big on bigness, went
with the original, but left it to Illyrians
to refine, whose light javelin turned up
in India next. Not for nothing were the
British Bengal Lancers feared and loathed.
Only the Bedouins might have given them
a run for their money. And on and on until
today, where it is mainly used for spearing fish.

Moment of Desire

4:32 A.M.

I always knew I had
the capacity to become
naked

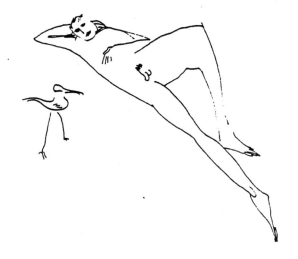

My Famous
Party-Giving
Guide

What to Wear

Fringed, fuchsia thing?

The Guest List

Joe
Ernie
Mabel
Harry
Sue
Anyone who is a plumber

Catering

Every plumber knows
at least one caterer.
But I say this is
America and that a
person's religion is his
or her own affair.
(Except if they are Jewish)

Invitations

Don't overspend. Hallmark is
unquestionably desirable, but this
is not the time to go haywire with
those costly extras. It is altogether
acceptable to contact your intended
guests by telephone. Allow them
reasonable time to make their replies
known to you. Be prepared to cope
with delays and disappointments.
After all, it was your idea to give
a party. Don't bear grudges. For
every seeming discourtesy there
must be an explanation. (This does
not necessarily mean you have to take
any shit from anybody.)

The Kitchen

There comes a time
when a hostess must
sit down and take a good
hard look at things.
Perhaps the floor-plan
is all wrong. Perhaps your
work space needs a redo
from the bottom up. Some
hostesses discover there
is a certain built-in
drawback to having a party.
But this is not the time
for negativism. How far
away is the nearest Burger
King? Pizza Hut? Or
Good Humor Man?

The Table

Must be big enough so
all may sit comfortably.
It is especially important
guests be far enough distanced
from one another not to be
needlessly bothered by the odd fart.

Hats

I adore this category! You
know those shiny things that
come to a point? Chin-straps
should be good and sturdy.

Seating

Needs lots of thought.
Here is where so many
party-givers miss the
boat. What takes
precedence as far as
making up your mind who
sits next to who?
Look, lets face it,
put Sue next to the
plumber. Period!

Tableware

I recognize a myriad of
perspectives bear on the
resolution of this
particular amenity. But I,
Enid, brush them aside and
say, with perfect conviction
and finality, the spork! It's
direct. It's honest. It
gets the job done, and, by
golly, it's darned good fun.

Beverage

A hearty quenching of
one's thirst is essential
to the well-managed
function. Olden Times or
any decent bourbon should
do. As for when the guests
arrive, and how best to
satisfy *their* thirst, don't
risk anything cut-rate.
In other words, economy-size
Shasta soda, in certain
on-sale flavors, is right
on the money. But lemon-
lime is absolutely out.
Ice cubes should be frosty
and dirt-free.

Balloons

There are endless options available to the
sensible, hospitality-minded hostess, but
let's not be completely ridick about it.

Noisemakers

I'll cover this later,
but if Harry isn't coming,
then what to do when those
awful lulls develop? For
develop they will! Horns,
whistles, and rubber bands
can help. But use in
moderation. Remember the
rule, "Have fun, but don't
look Jewish."

Napkins

No hostess should be
embarrassed by the
character of her decision
in this department. Ask
yourself this question—
"How long a walk is it,
after all, to the kitchen
sink?" And remember, Joe
is wearing fresh, clean,
naturally absorbent clothing.

Crêpe Paper

Yes! Yes! Yes! Yes!

The Greeting

Don't tarry. Be dressed and ready to go.
Once that doorbell rings, it's too late for
a sanitary napkin, ladies! Early arrivers
will have to be dealt with, but be sympathetic.
Remember Harry's operation. Don't forget—
these are your guests, these are friends, and
none of them are Jewish.

Centerpiece

All right, we come to that
most thorny of questions—
"What exactly is a centerpiece?"

Flowers

Here's where you can really shine. Go
all out. Don't spare the horses. The right
floral treatment can make or break your party.
Think color scheme, think wallpaper, think
draperies, think tablecloth! Remember, you're
wearing fuchsia, right? Now God be with you.

Pilfering

It all depends.
If Mabel falls asleep,
and has let go of her
handbag, then okay,
go ahead.

Liability Insurance

Only if it's too late to
get back in touch with
Harry in time.

Hors d'oeuvres

Pets, yes—but there is no
reason to turn this thing
into some kind of barnyard,
is there?

Diplomacy

If the plumber says it's the Jews, then it's the Jews!

Aperitif

Manischewitz.

What to Feed Them

Butt Cake.

Choking

From time to time—do not be alarmed—this
will occur. Another reason to cross Harry off.

Serving

Don't people
have two feet?

Music

Something light. Nothing too
pushy or Jewish.

Security

A crucial consideration.
Be on guard. Be alert.
Never neglect the likelihood
that things can get out of
control. People have a
tendency to be carried away.
Do your best to curb the
brutal instincts as they
break out over the course of
the evening's divertisement.
In this regard, probably best
to give a handjob to the
plumber *before* Joe.

What if Someone Falls?

Do not move this person until
you have determined who it is.
Yes, it's probably Harry. But
it's always better to act with
judgment and care. Moving
a fallen human being can result
in a fatality and a potential lawsuit.
Be creative. Stop and think. Could
this be an opportunity for that all
important subject—philosophy? For
example, "How much Butt Cake can
anyone eat?"

Lighting

Definitely subdued and
romantic and flattering.
On the other hand, provide
for sufficient illumination
to discourage Mabel from
thinking she can pocket her spork.

Having Fun

A must.
I always recommend
observing the traditional
values when it comes to
enlivening the party with
small, modest entertainments.
It could happen that one of the
guests would like to sing. Joe,
for instance. But if Joe should be
unwilling to give of himself, don't
despair. There's always someone who's
happy to pitch in. Perhaps Ernie would
be agreeable to showing everyone his anus.

Weapons

Yes, you should have one.

Conversation

You might have thought of
this before you made up
your guest list!

Use of the Facilities

Not on your life!

Preparing the Powder Room

Nothing more promptly exhibits
the tone of your welcome than the
pains taken before hand. Some
say a saucer placed on an
easy-to-reach table is the right
touch. Years of experience,
however, have convinced me to suggest
it is better to post a sign—a
paper plate will do nicely—on the
bathroom door. There is debate as
to the best approach concerning its
language. Myself, I still favor the
simple, plain, old-fashioned solution—
OUT OF ORDER: KEEP THE FUCK OUT!

Games

Planet Comics puts out
a wonderful and attractively
priced book of crossword
puzzles. But if your budget
has been strained to the
limit, I usually recommend
quoits or Ernie.

Staffing the Kitchen

Definitely! Definitely!
But bear in mind the
customary precautions.
It's a question of weighing
good, clean, honest fun
against perversion and
disease.

Chaining the Dog

On second thought, it's
probably a better idea to
belt the plumber to his chair.

The Search

Your guests
need not be exposed
to rough handling or
to a state of undress.
It is perfectly suitable,
and should cause no one any
dismay, for you to pat them
down as they make their
way to the door. Remember,
you have furnished food and
entertainment. Fair is fair.

The Farewell

You're a big girl! It's high
time you knew how to say good-bye
without constantly depending on
little me for advice.

What to do with Leftovers

You silly you. You don't
have to do *any*thing with
leftovers.

Afterglow

Time to sit back and
congratulate yourself on
a job well done. Chew
a stick of gum.

TEN COMPOSITIONS
ELEVEN

— BY FRANK

914 S. 5th ST #3

Milwaukee, WI 53204

(414) 672-5023

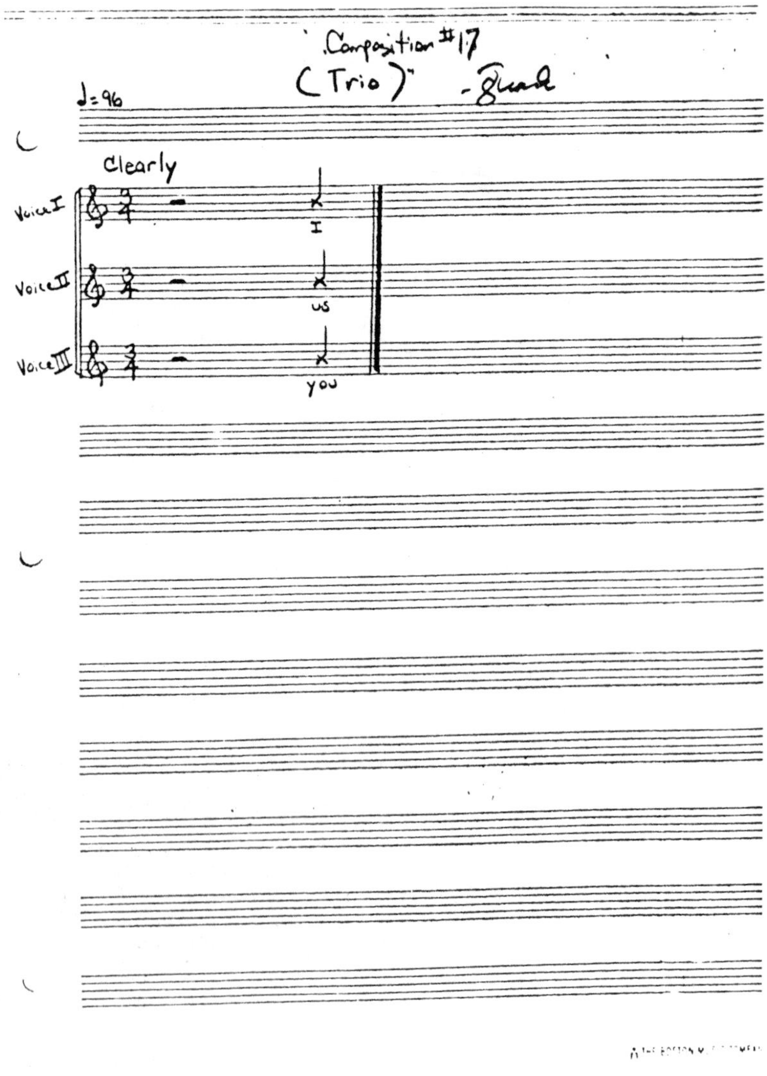
"Composition #17
(Trio)"
♩=96
Clearly
Voice I
Voice II
Voice III
I
us
you

* Trumpet may use circular breathing.

** Performance lasts 6 years, so bring
ample clothes and food.

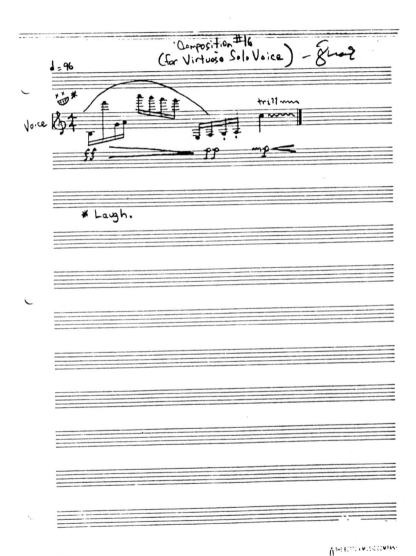

* Laugh.

Composition #14
(For Solo Voice)

♩ = 272

Make it last

Voice

pp

THE BOSTON MUSIC COMPANY

Composition #5
(unfinished)

Composition #4
(for Two Voices)

Voice I
Hey,

Voice II
(repeat as necessary)

THE BOSTON MUSIC COMPANY

Composition #15
(for Ensemble)

* Watch conductor,
look for direction.

* to be performed 10:30 a.m./Mondays.

Dear mr. Lish,

Want a page in your magazine. I Nawt one real bad, like a Page just for ME in every "Q" from now on. Please?!? PAGE 172 (cause 1+7+2 = 10 = my favorite NUMBer). I promise to not really mess up the whole Q for Everyone like I have other Things.

— Thank (writer)

P.S. or 173 (1 x 7 + 3 = 10) !!

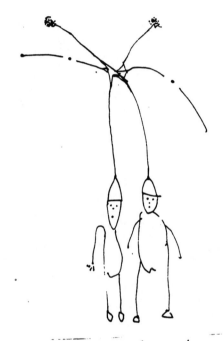

I caught someone staring at me

FOR ORDERS OF BACK NUMBERS, SEE PRICES AND ISBN CODES SHOWN BELOW
AND CONTACT SUBSCRIPTION OFFICE. NOTE ADDITION OF POSTAGE AND HANDLING
CHARGE AT $1.50 THE COPY PER EACH COPY REQUESTED.

Q1	$6.95	394-74697-x	Q15	$8.95	679-73231-4
Q2	$6.95	394-74698-8	Q16	$8.95	679-73244-6
Q3	$6.95	394-75536-7	Q17	$10.00	679-73494-5
Q4	$6.95	394-75537-5	Q18	$10.00	679-73495-3
Q5	$6.95	394-75718-1	Q19	$10.00	679-73690-5
Q6	$6.95	394-75719-x	Q20	$10.00	679-73691-3
Q7	$6.95	394-75936-2	Q21	$10.00	679-73862-2
Q8	$6.95	394-75937-0	Q22	$10.00	679-73050-3
Q9	$6.95	679-72139-8	Q23	$10.00	679-74224-7
Q10	$6.95	679-72172-x	Q24	$10.00	679-74225-5
Q11	$6.95	679-72173-8	Q25	$10.00	679-74501-7
Q12	$6.95	679-72153-3	Q26	$10.00	969-6520-4-6
Q13	$8.95	679-72743-4	Q27	$10.00	969-6520-5-4
Q14	$8.95	679-72893-7	Q28	$10.00	969-6520-7-0

To the eeitor

XØ̶X̶X̶H̶ẞ̶X̶is driving me crazy. Up all ᴋg
night. You can¢t even lock the t₋i-
lets in this place. in case youwant to
ᴋᴀ ᴋᴀᴀᴋknow Ξnid J Crackel steals of h
her recipes from More Joy of cooking.
Alos, she spi̶t̶ s in everything she cᴏcks
.

    I have recommended Enid J Crackel f
᷍or electoshock therapy but so far n᷍
one has respondid to my suggesti on.
Perhaps they,slong with the ra᷍t fo the
world feel my opihi᷍n is ᷍f now wor th.
    I h᷍ve tried wth all my ᷍e᷍t᷍ ᷍ h᷍
ᴌᴵ᷍ J Crackel.
    ᶁᴋᴤᴜᴊᴋᴜᴀᴤᶁᴇ̶ᴊᴄᴄᴊᴊᴌᴜᴋᴋᴋᴋᴋᴋᴧᶁᴋ the
mamby pandry poems you now publish upᴘ
on the public domain. You are walking
the path of the dammed.

Cordually

County Home for the Aged

PS Ξᴋᴀᴊ Enid has hiar on her ass.